100 ESSENTIAL NEW ZEALAND Films

Hamish McDouall

100 ESSENTIAL NEW ZEALAND Films

AWA PRESS

First published in 2009 by Awa Press,
16 Walter Street, Wellington, New Zealand.

For illustration credits, see pages 248–53.

A CIP catalogue record for this book is available from the National Library of New Zealand.

ISBN 978-0-9582750-9-5

Illustrations on previous pages: half title page – Len Lye, *A Colour Box* (1935); title page Keisha Castle-Hughes in *Whale Rider*.

Book design by Fortyfive Design, Wellington
Typeset by Jenn Hadley, Wellington
Printed by Everbest Printing Company, China
This book is typeset in Minion

www.awapress.com

Produced with the assistance of

creative nz
ARTS COUNCIL OF NEW ZEALAND TOI AOTEAROA

This book is dedicated to the memory
of my late sister-in-law Denys McDouall
(née Fotheringham), who loved the cinema.

Contents

Contents

Introduction

'Are there a hundred?' This was the almost universal response when I mentioned I was writing this book. It would be followed by a list of features – *Smash Palace, In My Father's Den, The Piano, Once Were Warriors, Came A Hot Friday, Rain, Footrot Flats.* Then a pause. 'Have you seen *Second-Hand Wedding?*' 'Are you counting *Lord Of The Rings* as one film or three?' 'Is *King Kong* a New Zealand film?' I would explain that shorts and documentaries were included, and the uncategorisable works of Len Lye. As the concept sunk in there would be other comments. Had I seen *A Game With No Rules? Kitchen Sink? Two Cars, One Night?* The one about the demolition derby in the far north?

These conversations would take place on buses, in lounges and cafes, on the telephone. Sometimes strange and virtually unknown films would be mentioned, or films in which the people themselves were involved. One thing stood out: although New Zealand films have won Oscars, Palmes d'Or and numerous other awards at international film festivals, there is still a cringe factor. Several times people said, 'Not bad for a Kiwi film,' as if it were necessary to give more latitude to the local product. People no longer say that about Janet Frame's novels, Colin McCahon's paintings, or the latest album from Fat Freddy's Drop. Let's hope that after reading this book they will stop saying it about New Zealand films.

A book of this kind is always going to be, to some degree, subjective. There are films I excluded capriciously. I saw *Brain-*

dead alongside a packed audience of merry students when I was twenty-three. It was hilarious and I loved it. I saw *Bad Taste* sober, alone and ten years later. I hated it. I make no apologies for not including it or *Footrot Flats* or *Mauri* or *The Ugly*, even though you will find earnest champions of these films. On the other hand, I have included several films I didn't personally enjoy: I could see that by the most rational of criteria they had to be deemed 'essential'.

Finally, I often cursed the tyranny of the 100: many films missed by the mere width of a frame. At another time, with the wind blowing in a different direction, any one of these would be worthy of a place: *Bread And Roses, Snail's Pace, The Return, Twilight Of The Gods, Sons For The Return Home, Sylvia, Permanent Wave, Woman At The Store, Kissy Kissy, Gordon Bennett, Changing Of The Guard, Uso, Whole Of The Moon, Starlight Hotel, 9 Across, Irene 59, Their Town, Junk* and *The Story Of Wonder What*. I hope readers will take this book as a starting point to explore, discover and rediscover the many treasures of New Zealand cinema.

– Hamish McDouall

An Angel At My Table

THE PIANO MAY HAVE WON THE GONGS, and *Sweetie* may have been nominated for a Palme d'Or and scored an Australian Film Institute award, but *An Angel At My Table*, a distillation of author Janet's Frame's three-volume autobiography, is Jane Campion's greatest achievement.

It is a staggering work. Campion worked on a relatively limited budget – the project was intended as a three-part miniseries for television but edited together for cinema release. This gives it an intimacy, with tight compositions that enhance the feeling of a close-knit family living in modest circumstances, but limits the opportunities for expansive set pieces and other cinematic indulgences. *An Angel At My Table* still manages to feel like an epic at times, but at heart it is a record of a life lived, bad teeth and all.

Although the story is necessarily long, extending from Frame's childhood to her early thirties, it is never tedious. Each episode illuminates, little by little, the process of how a flame-haired infant became one of New Zealand's greatest writers. There is real joy in the scenes of the four Frame sisters, and a sense that Janet's imagination was fired by the magic of childhood, reading vivid books, befriending a girl who claims to be Spanish, making fun in the woods, listening to a teacher quoting poetry.

Kerry Fox's performance is brilliant, not least for the fact that she put on twelve kilograms for the role – mainly through Coca-

Cola, chocolate biscuits and the pill. There is a heaviness in her movements and a candour in the minutiae of her expressions. The scenes in Seacliff mental hospital, where 200 doses of electroshock therapy were inflicted on Frame, may be the most traumatic, but Fox is equally capable when displaying the writer's debilitating shyness, her heartbreaking grief at the death of her sister Myrtle, her confusion at romantic attentions in Ibiza. She is often viewed gazing at worlds barred to her – Myrtle's last extravagant dance, the popular group at college, the bohemian crowd in Ibiza.

The other Janets (Alexia Keogh and Karen Fergusson) should also be mentioned in despatches, but it is hard to identify a single cast member who doesn't put in a top performance – especially Glynis Angell, Martyn Sanderson, Melina Bernecker and Iris Churn.

Stuart Dryburgh again shows his mastery at lighting a film – the scene of little Janet at the end of a farm road has become cinematic shorthand for New Zealand cinema. The music by Don McGlashan

An Angel At My Table
1990 / Feature / 152 mins

DIRECTOR / **Jane Campion**
PRODUCER / **Bridget Ikin**
SCREENPLAY / **Laura Jones**
PRODUCTION COMPANY / **Hibiscus Films**

is lilting and upbeat, and gentle humour throughout the script alleviates the harrowing sequences. But Jane Campion's real triumph is her ability to condense enormous personal moments into small details. In a memorable example, we are not given a graphic depiction of electroshock therapy, just shown Janet's feet tensing as it is carried out.

Renowned New York film critic Danny Peary, in his book *Alternate Oscars*, declared *An Angel At My Table* 1991's best film. If pushed and prodded I might declare it the finest feature film ever made in New Zealand.

Angel Mine

DAVID BLYTH HAS GIVEN NEW ZEALAND CINEMA some extraordinary images – the brain surgery in *Death Warmed Up*, the aerial beach sequence in *Grampire*, the disturbing vignettes in webcam documentary *Transfigured Nights*. He is also responsible for the moment in *Circadian Rhythms* when Derek Ward removes his penis and tosses it on the ground, perhaps the most startling scene in New Zealand cinema history.

Blyth watched Luis Buñuel's *Un Chien Andalou* fifty times before making *Circadian Rhythms*. That its follow-up, *Angel Mine*, owes a debt to the Spaniard's later work – most particularly *The Discreet Charm Of The Bourgeoisie* and *Phantom Of Liberty* – is evident from the first scene, when a sailor emerges from the surf and dresses a naked woman who is sitting primly on a toilet in the sand.

The plot, what there is of it, involves a middle-class couple who live alienated from each other, with television and advertising filling the void. Their rimu-panelled home sits in a treeless cul-de-sac. They are hunted by leather-clad doppelgangers, who describe in ultra-violent terms how they will kill them.

When the New Zealand Film Commission was founded in 1978, *Angel Mine* was the first film to receive funding. When a prominent wowser, Patricia Bartlett, questioned why taxpayers' money was being spent on such an explicit and controversial project, the censor devised a special classification: 'Contains Punk Cult Material'.

Angel Mine
1978 / Feature / 67 mins

DIRECTOR / SCREENPLAY /
David Blyth
PRODUCERS / **David Blyth, Warren Sellers**
PRODUCTION COMPANY /
ILA Productions

Angel Mine has dated, occasionally very badly, and the humour is often sophomoric – Blyth was just twenty-two when he made it – but some of the satire remains impressive, particularly when the 'advertising' intrudes. A nun advertises for abortions, Captain Hotshot (Mike Wilson) leaps out of a closet to sodomise the leading man, and Death enjoys a beer after finishing the lawns. There is also a wildly funny scene where a woman gets aroused while on talkback radio, and a fabulous ballet involving a clothesline.

As the censor detected, *Angel Mine* has something of a punk aesthetic: it can feel as if the plot is evolving while being filmed. Consumerism, conformity and boredom are despised and figuratively murdered. Suburban Reptiles' surging 'Saturday Night Stay At Home' features. And New Zealand's first punk concert raised funds for it.

Avondale Dogs

JUST AS NEW ZEALAND has produced world-class short-story writers such as Katherine Mansfield, Frank Sargeson, Janet Frame, Witi Ihimaera, Owen Marshall and Emily Perkins, it has produced short-film-makers who similarly build resonances from small details and concise episodes to attain an emotional apex.

Avondale Dogs is such a work – one of the most assured and powerful short films made in New Zealand. If there is a disappointment it is that the director, Gregor Nicholas, has not made more films. Since his second feature, *Broken English*, was released just two years later there has been cinematic silence.

Avondale Dogs, impressionistic and autobiographical, relates the experience of a boy growing up in a suburban Auckland cul-de-sac in the 1950s. The detail – hurricane mesh fences, treeless yards and state houses – suggests the austerity of the place and time perfectly, while black and white cinematography gives the film a nostalgic, dream-like quality. This is memory being replicated on screen.

Paul (Daniel Lay) is nearing puberty but far from fully comprehending what he is experiencing. His mother (Rhondda Findleton) is dying, and when Paul sneaks a BB gun out of his father's cupboard to shoot birds, he connects his guilt about killing a pigeon to the worsening of his mother's illness.

There are wonderful scenes. Paul has a crush on Glenys, the Maori girl next door, and in a smoke-shed the pair catch drips

Avondale Dogs
1994 / Short / 15 mins

DIRECTOR / SCREENPLAY /
Gregor Nicholas
PRODUCER / Stephanie Bauer
PRODUCTION COMPANY /
This Is It

from hanging eels in their mouths. Then there is the palpable grief of Paul's father at the hospital, and the image that gives the movie its title: dogs eating pies from a crashed delivery truck.

The film's great strength is its understatement: Nicholas was heavily influenced by the movies of Japanese director Yasujiro Ozu (*Tokyo Monogatari, Banshun*) – simple, compassionate, restrained stories of ordinary people. The camera is static. Music is largely absent, apart from Debussy's *Prelude*, which opens the film, and the funeral waiata that closes it. The characters are downplayed. The climax when Paul places a shoplifted ring on Glenys's finger, suggesting a love that will transcend the time of trauma, is fully worthy of Ozu.

Baby Farmer

48HOURS, an annual film-making contest, challenges teams to create, shoot and edit a short film in two days. They are given a genre, a prop, a character and a line of dialogue, and then it's open slather. Oscar nominees compete with unknowns, corporate film-makers with rank amateurs, and over the competition weekend there is hardly a street corner in a main city that is not occupied by a small film crew.

The results are often patchy but sometimes witty, hilarious or comically surreal. Drama and subtlety are rare as film-makers are aware of their audience, a horde of their own friends who are usually euphoric, uninhibited, and wanting to laugh.

This makes Sam Kelly's taut and thoughtful horror *Baby Farmer* all the more remarkable. Not only was it conceived, acted and photographed with professional skill within 48 hours, it also managed to silence a boisterous boozy audience with its mastery of horror conventions.

The story is simple. A man is seeking to buy a house for his mistress. The couple views a colonial house that was once owned by Southland's most famous criminal, Minnie Dean, convicted and hanged for murdering babies at the end of the nineteenth century. As well as a sense of disquiet induced by the house's ominously lit corridors and ramshackle staircase, there is tension between the couple. The woman is pregnant and Robin Slade, played with

Baby Farmer
2006 / Short / 7 mins

DIRECTOR / Sam Kelly
PRODUCER / Bonnie Slater
PRODUCTION COMPANY / Team Good Times

arrogance and malevolence by Phil Vaughan, is demanding she get an abortion: 'I've got my own family.' Then a mirror catches a fleeting spectral reflection – it is evident the couple are not alone.

This is unapologetically a horror film, but the dénouement is not just terrifying but tender, a perfect and improbable moment of catharsis.

Baby Farmer won the Wellington heat of the 2006 contest and came second in the popular vote nationwide, but the quality of its film-making means it transcended its origins and was shown at 'real' film festivals. That the film stands up alongside shorts with bigger budgets and months of planning is a tribute to Kelly and his cast and crew – and to 48Hours for encouraging anarchic creativity to flourish.

Bad Blood

BAD BLOOD TELLS THE STORY of the 1941 killing spree by West Coaster Stanley Graham, and the manhunt that followed. The subject matter is similar to 2006's *Out Of The Blue*, but whereas in that film the landscape is benign and the violence an aberration, the landscape in *Bad Blood* is full of threat and entrapment. The film was made where the tragic events occurred and the hedged farmhouse has a gothic bleakness. In most exterior shots the Southern Alps loom through the mist. Regular downpours add to the sense of claustrophobia.

This is not a story of man against nature, but of a couple ostracised and made paranoid by the community around them. There are parallels between this community, Koiterangi, and the Aramoana of *Out Of The Blue*, but Stanley Graham is not the sociopath David Gray was. It is bad luck, a simmering dispute with neighbours, and the difficult wartime economy that have isolated the Grahams and poisoned not only their thoughts but, they believe, their milk.

The study of the once close-knit community is compelling. War and poverty are pulling it apart, leaving holes in the fabric for the Grahams to slip through. Dot Graham is from Christchurch and feels like an outsider. Gossip stops when she enters a shop; she is addressed with bland phatic by the other residents. The laconic Stan seems to wear a constant sadness. Love is evident between

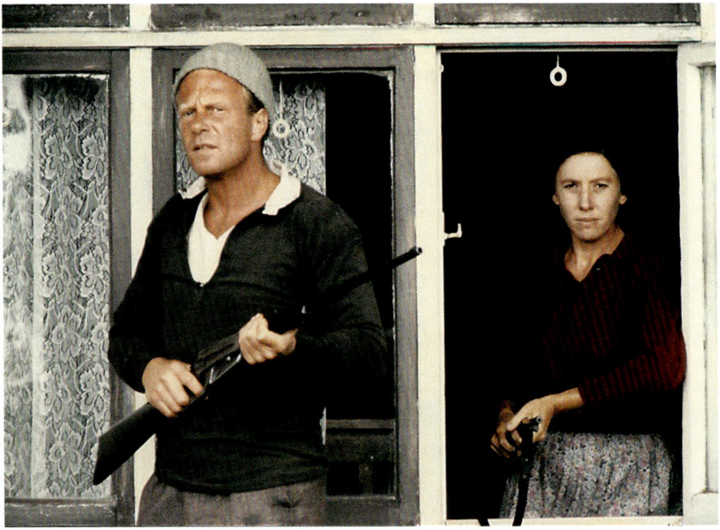

the besieged pair, but their night-time target practice is unsettling, suggesting a brewing insanity. When police come to confiscate the couple's rifles for the war effort, the massacre begins. The shootings are not shown in a stylised way: this is visceral realism, and the violence is fast and confusing.

Bad Blood treads a fine balance, neither demonising Graham nor lionising him. While it is easy to feel sympathy for him as he is hunted, the grittiness of the shootings and the death of Ted Best remind us that this is murder. There is similar ambivalence towards the community. The Grahams' alienation seems to have its source in the town's pettiness and prejudice, yet when a local man is killed in action the people bond in grief. Interestingly, the macho posturing of the organised search party is undercut when Graham returns and kills again: it is now the community that is paranoid.

Bad Blood
1981 / Feature / 113 mins

DIRECTOR / Mike Newell
PRODUCER / SCREENPLAY / Andrew Brown
PRODUCTION COMPANY / Southern Pictures

This is the only film in this book not directed by a New Zealander. Englishman Mike Newell (*Four Weddings And A Funeral*) was hired because the film was largely financed by a British company, Southern Pictures. The leads, Jack Thompson and Carol Burns, are Australian. However, this is indubitably a New Zealand film, with one of the strongest local casts ever assembled. Donna Akersten, Marshall Napier, Martyn Sanderson, John Bach, Pat Evison, Miranda Harcourt, Dorothy McKegg, Ian Watkin, Bruce Allpress and Kelly Johnson all have supporting roles, and the quality of the ensemble work is remarkable.

Beautiful...

TWO BLOKES, BARRY AND KEV, go fishing in a dinghy on Great Barrier Island's Port Fitzroy harbour. The landscape is picturesque, the scenery glowing. It's 'fucking beautiful', Barry thinks.

The men chat idly as the bait is prepared and lures set. When Barry mentions that he slaps his wife around, there is silence. Then Kev rocks the boat: 'Why do you never slap me a bit?'

Based on a skit by a comedy duo called Sugar and Spice, *Beautiful...* is an exploration of the sexual no-man's-land between 'red-blooded' mates. Following the classic prescription for creating

drama, it puts two people in a confined space and throws in a large measure of discomfort. The humour, initially directed at the boorish misogynist Barry, changes to a squirming kind of comedy.

Beautiful...
2001 / Short / 12 mins
DIRECTOR / SCREENPLAY / **Adam Stevens**
PRODUCER / **Mark Foster**
PRODUCTION COMPANY / **Whippersnapper**

Beautiful's script, particularly a monologue about bisexuality being au courant, is tight and funny. Tim Gordon (*Fracture, For Good*) excels as the homophobic Barry, but the film relies on the ambiguity and timing of Jason Hoyte (*We're Here To Help, Outrageous Fortune*), reprising his stage role as Kev, who just fancies pashing another fella. This film gained international attention, being selected for both Sundance and New York film festivals.

Beyond Reasonable Doubt

BASED ON DAVID YALLOP'S BOOK about the infamous 1970 murder of Waikato farming couple Jeanette and Harvey Crewe and the subsequent trial of their neighbour Arthur Allan Thomas, this film has two very different parts. The first follows the discovery of the Crewes' baby in their abandoned, blood-stained farmhouse, and the police investigation that follows. Once Thomas has been arrested, the film morphs into a thrilling courtroom drama.

In the opening sequence two people enter an empty house and discover a baby girl. She is alive and well-fed, but there are sinister signs. Soon the parents' disappearance is being investigated

and the film becomes both a police procedural story and the study of a small rural community, which reveals itself in tiny, telling details.

Beyond Reasonable Doubt
1980 Feature 113 mins
DIRECTOR John Laing
PRODUCER John Barnett
SCREENPLAY David Yallop
PRODUCTION COMPANY
Endeavour Productions

The script consistently undercuts our expectations of the characters. Inspector Bruce Hutton (David Hemmings) begins as a forceful investigator keen to find the truth, but becomes a pragmatist willing to plant evidence to gain a conviction. Jeanette Crewe's father Len Demler (Martyn Sanderson) initially seems cold-hearted and suspicious but comes to seem just naturally gruff.

Australian John Hargreaves (*Cry Freedom, Hotel Sorrento*), cast for his likeness to Thomas, is brilliant. His naïve wonder, willingness to help and stammering delivery perfectly capture the essence of a country hick caught in a vortex beyond his comprehension.

There have never been better courtroom scenes in New Zealand cinema. Ian Watkin (*Wild Man, Braindead*) plays barrister Kevin Ryan with stentorian bluster, while Grant Tilly (*Carry Me Back, Middle Age Spread*) affects a hearty Scottish brogue for his role as the Crown solicitor, David Morris.

This is not a perfect film. The courtroom sequences seem hurried and some threads of the plot are left frayed. There was, however, a valid reason for the rush. In 1979, when *Beyond Reasonable Doubt* was in post-production, it was proved that the police had planted evidence and Arthur Allan Thomas was granted a pardon. The final scene, in which Hargreaves, as Thomas, returns home, was filmed with Thomas's real family on his Pukekawa farm.

Blue Willow

IN NEW ZEALAND, animation is pursued mostly in the short film, no doubt because of the craft's expense and time-hungry demands. Other than Murray Ball's 1986 *Footrot Flats: The Dog's Tale*, there have been no serious attempts at feature-length animation.

Many short animated films may have made it into this book had space permitted: Sebastian Doyle's *The Grocer's Apprentice*, with its brilliant stop-action and sinister Tiny Teddies; Guy Capper's witty *The Pen*; Tom Reilly's claymation *Man With Issues*; Fred O'Neill's combinations of play dough and Maori legend for several National Film Unit films; and *I Believe In Ewe*, a wonderful 2D fairy tale by a group called The Perfcetionists, shown only once at the 48Hours film-making contest. But there is something about *Blue Willow*, its handling of political and personal, myth and reality, and the pull of different cultures, that makes it rise above the rest.

The film invokes the story of the Chinese legend that inspired the Blue Willow plate, engraved by Englishman Thomas Minton in the eighteenth century and produced by Royal Doulton, Spode, Wedgwood and countless other companies since. Over the years, willow pattern china has become a part of Kiwiana, and this cross-over of myth to kitsch interested director Veialu Aila-Unsworth. 'It still makes me laugh,' she wrote, 'to think that such an elegant plate, with such a beautiful story, would find itself being smothered by leftover macaroni cheese or fish pie.'

Simplicity in both art and script are the keys to her magical, dream-like film. The viewer enters a blue and white world where a noblewoman, Koong-se, has been promised by her father to a bellicose warrior duke, Ta-jin, in spite of her love for a commoner, Chang. Koong-se's grief is vividly and elegantly portrayed as her sapphire tears turn into golden butterflies.

Blue Willow
2005 / Short / 14 mins

DIRECTOR / PRODUCER / SCREENPLAY / **Veialu Aila-Unsworth**

The animation is deliberately crude and childlike to reflect the fact that Aila-Unsworth was told the story as a young girl. There is a sublime string score by Timothy Beals, a nice surprise ending, and a marvellous sketched dragon that consumes the two lovers.

This visionary film screened in competition at the Berlin Film Festival, and has since been shown at a score of film festivals in places as diverse as Quebec, Kenya and Wairoa.

Braindead

YOU WILL NOT FIND PETER JACKSON'S FIRST FEATURE, *Bad Taste,* in this book. It may have almost singlehandedly spawned a new genre, splatter comedy ('splatstick') and launched Jackson, both as Derek and behind the camera, towards the stratosphere, but the occasional one-liner, exploding sheep and spot of do-it-yourself brain surgery do not make up for the amateur acting, muddled screenplay, and monotony of the shoot-'em-up climax.

Braindead (renamed *Dead Alive* for American audiences) perfected what *Bad Taste* began. With high production values and an even higher body count, it purrs like a well-fed Sumatran rat-monkey from the moment Stewart (Bill Ralston) has his arm amputated in the first reel. The plot, a secondary feature, involves a closeted Norman Bates-ish lad (Tim Balme), his homicidal mother (Elizabeth Moody), a Spanish love interest (Diana Peñalver), and a load of zombies.

Braindead is gory, gripping and so over-the-top that censors in Britain and Australia did not cut a single scene. Tongues, when not being ripped out and eaten by the undead, are firmly in cheeks. The humour always overwhelms the horror, although it sometimes walks a thin tightrope – most notably when, during the visit of a vicar, blood and pus get mixed with scones and clotted cream. The details of 1950s New Zealand domestic ordinariness – Aunt Daisy, porcelain wall ducks, Kiwi bacon – enhance the anarchy.

The visual jokes, particularly the pram with the wire grill, are delicious. Some of the one-liners (and most of the limbs) come off.

The climactic battle of zombies versus Uncle Les (Ian Watkin) and the young couple armed with a garden gnome, Rinso soap powder and a lawnmower required tonnes of maple syrup and food colouring. During the lawnmower scene this 'blood' was pumped at five gallons a second. Not surprisingly, *Braindead* has been listed as the bloodiest movie of all time on Internet Movie Database.

Braindead
1992 / Feature / 95 mins

DIRECTOR / **Peter Jackson**
PRODUCER / **James Booth**
SCREENPLAY / **Fran Walsh, Peter Jackson, Stephen Sinclair**
PRODUCTION COMPANY / **WingNut Films**

Broken Barrier

BETWEEN 1940 AND 1964 only one fiction feature film was produced in New Zealand. *Broken Barrier* was made on a shoestring using two mute cameras, one on loan from Movietone News and the other, according to director John O'Shea, 'taken from a dead German soldier in the Western Desert'.

O'Shea and Roger Mirams, his partner in Pacific Films, had come from the National Film Unit, which produced the earnestly drawn slices of life that were *Weekly Review*. Both men were also fans of the Italian neo-realism of Roberto Rossellini and Vittorio De Sica. It is no surprise, then, that there is a strong sense of the documentary about *Broken Barrier*: the stentorian voice-over ('These people are Maoris') and careful images of a group gathering kai moana could come from an ethnographic short. Spontaneous real-life incidents (such as a strangely tame bird) and events (an All Black test match) are incorporated into the narrative.

The story itself is an oft-told tale: love in the face of prejudice. Terence Bayler plays Tom, a tabloid journalist who, in search of an exploitative scoop, goes to Mahia Peninsula pretending to seek work. Instead he finds love with Rawi (Kay Ngarimu) amid rustling grasses. However, Rawi's parents are unhappy about the interracial relationship, and cultural differences quickly become evident.

On Tom's return to Wellington he tries to rekindle the relationship, but the racism of his family and friends again drives the lovers apart. It will take an ill-fated friendship with a Maori man while he is working as a timber worker for Tom to realise how much he cares for Rawi.

Broken Barrier
1952 / Feature / 71 mins

DIRECTORS / PRODUCERS / John O'Shea, Roger Mirams
SCREENPLAY / John O'Shea
PRODUCTION COMPANY / Pacific Films

Cash constraints meant *Broken Barrier* was shot without sound: the characters tell their stories through the disconcerting vehicle of voice-overs. There is a paternalism that grates, an earnestness that wears heavily, and a rather too idealistic dénouement. Nevertheless, *Broken Barrier* tackled the national myth of racial harmony square on, and is an endearing, bittersweet film.

Came A Hot Friday

THIS HOT WESTERLY GUST OF A FILM contains some of the most memorable comic performances by New Zealand actors. Peter Bland is Wes Pennington, a con man who, with his offsider Cyril Kidman (Phillip Gordon), thrives on stinging bookies. Pennington is loquacious, witty and scheming. Kidman is slick and shallow; he shoots his cuffs regularly, and dances like a down-under Fred Astaire. That the duo requires the help of the Tainuia Kid (Billy T. James), a bona fide lunatic who believes he is a Mexican bandito, tells you much about their success.

Came A Hot Friday was adapted from a novel by Ronald Hugh Morrieson, but some of the book's darker hues were excised and its comic parts enhanced. Shot in south Taranaki, where Morrieson lived, the film's production design and soundtrack are richly atmospheric. This is heartland New Zealand at the end of the 1940s, but with liberal dollops of lust and petty criminality.

There is barely a character who is not compromised, although the various scams and seductions seem small fry compared to the arson and murderous intent of the local casino operator Sel Bishop (Marshall Napier) and bookmaker Norm Clay (Don Selwyn). Bishop and Clay's dogged pursuit of the shysters doesn't just add comic jeopardy: it makes for a sense of disquiet. These malicious and dangerous characters seem to belong to a much more sinister film.

There are problems with *Came A Hot Friday* that are not entirely blown away by the film's breezy tone. The movie seems overpopulated, and occasionally the chases descend into chaos. Some of the supporting acting is so poor you wonder if the secondary casting was done at a secondhand furniture store. Most of the female characters are drawn only as far as the hem of their skirts.

But the film is fondly remembered for its broad comedy. There are blasts of Mexitanga from Billy T. James, puns and one-liners from Peter Bland, and slapstick and pratfalls from just about everybody else. The second half is a frenetic blast, and the woolshed casino a memorable set piece.

Alun Bollinger's cinematography is, as always, eloquent, and there is a poignant last appearance by Prince Tui Teka playing saxophone, just before his untimely death. *Came A Hot Friday* also includes my nominee for the best line in New Zealand cinema – 'Buenos dias, e hoa!'

Came A Hot Friday
1985 / Feature / 105 mins

DIRECTOR / **Ian Mune**
PRODUCER / **Larry Parr**
SCREENPLAY / **Dean Parker, Ian Mune**
PRODUCTION COMPANY / **Mirage Films**

Produced at a time when the apexes of New Zealand cinema were serious dramas, and tax dodges fuelled many irredeemable projects, *Came A Hot Friday*, a confident, riotous comedy, seemed a statement the industry had come of age. The skills learnt in the 1970s had been honed.

The Coaster

IN THE LATE 1930s the Labour government extended an invitation to John Grierson, founder of the British documentary film movement, to visit New Zealand. It would prove to be a key moment: Grierson's report added to pressure to reorganise the Government Film Studios, and in 1941 the National Film Unit was formed under the aegis of the prime minister's office. One of the government's aims was to boost support for the war effort, and a regular newsreel, *Weekly Review*, documented war-related activities.

From 1946 the principal focus became the life of the ordinary working New Zealander, and Grierson's maxim that 'documentary should contain a creative treatment of actuality' inspired the unit's young film-makers. Grierson's short film *Night Mail*, which combined images of a steam train with W.H. Auden's rhythmic poetry, influenced nascent talents such as Margaret Thomson (*Railway Worker*), who stated that she knew the film shot by shot.

Night Mail also inspired Cecil Holmes, who made *The Coaster*. The merchant vessel *Breeze* sails from Wellington to Lyttelton and back up the coast to Wanganui to the accompaniment of Denis Glover's sensuous poem of the same name. As the ship cuts through a solid Cook Strait swell the soundtrack of the churning motor and the rhythms of the stevedores seem almost balletic. Coastal shipping – 'to work with the white-collared wave' – appears dramatic, even heroic.

The Coaster
1948 / Short / 10 mins

DIRECTOR / Cecil Holmes
PRODUCER / Stanhope Andrews
SCREENPLAY / Denis Glover
PRODUCTION COMPANY / New Zealand National

For many years, the Film Unit shaped how New Zealanders viewed their country. *This Valley, Their Town, First Two Years At School, The Railway Worker, Cookery Nook* and *Snowline Is Their Boundary* found art in the mundane. This glorification of the working man suited Holmes, a card-carrying communist. His next film *Fighting Back*, about the Carpenters' Union, riled both government and Federation of Labour. His affiliations were leaked to the media, and in the post-war 'reds under beds' climate, he was dismissed and left New Zealand soon after, never to return.

A Colour Box

THE STORY OF NEW ZEALAND FILM is full of innovators and original thinkers. People such as Bob Stenhouse, Peter Jackson and Florian Habicht have pushed the boundaries when it comes to making images and telling stories on screen. However, only one film-maker has invented a whole new way of creating moving pictures. Len Lye, born in Christchurch in 1901 and a pioneering artist before those three were born, achieved just that with his beautiful abstraction *A Colour Box*. Made as an advertisement for the Post Office, it is one of the most captivating commercials of all time.

Lye painted frame by frame on discarded clear film with just a soundtrack on one side. He called this process 'direct' film-making, and it was largely a response to the time and money it had taken to produce his earlier ethno-erotic animation *Tusalava*. Painting directly on to celluloid was so much cheaper, requiring neither a camera, fresh film stock nor a developing process. It was also so much faster: where *Tusalava* had taken three years to make, *A Colour Box* was largely painted over five days.

With such a minute 'canvas', Lye used fine-toothed combs to paint striated wavy lines, and a fish slice to achieve regularity with patterns of coloured dots. For a floating motif he used an airbrush and stencil. Long lines were painted the length of the film.

One of the most remarkable things about Lye's abstractions are

A Colour Box
1935 / Short / 3 mins

DIRECTOR / CONCEPT / **Len Lye**
PRODUCER / **John Grierson**
PRODUCTION COMPANY / **British Government Post Office Film Unit**

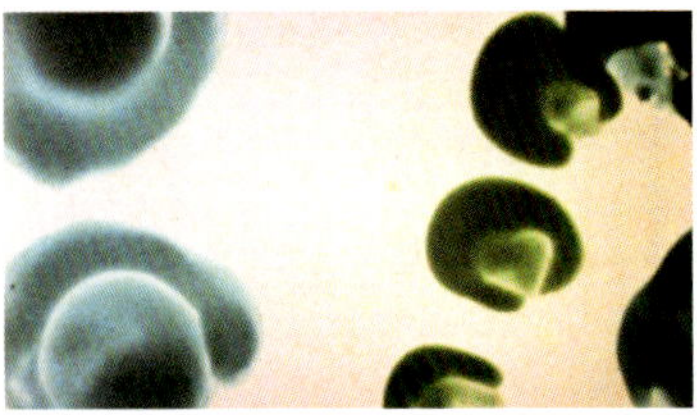

their synchronicity to the music, whether it be Tal Farlow's jazz or Sonny Terry's blues. With the help of an Australian composer, Jack Ellitt, Lye structured visual images to conform with the length of phrases and changes of orchestration. They chose the beguine 'La Belle Créole' by Don Baretto and his Cuban Orchestra for *A Colour Box*, then kept the images in step with the music while attempting never to be predictable.

In a world where films were still principally black and white, this burst of brilliant colour on screen must have been remarkable to experience, although it was not to everybody's taste. When the film was shown at the Venice Film Festival, it was booed by fascists: because it was an abstraction, the Nazi movement considered it entartete Kunst, degenerate art, and had organised a goon squad to show their displeasure.

Crush

CRUSH BEGINS WITH AN ASTONISHING CAR CRASH that interrupts a pretentious, highbrow conversation between the two women in the vehicle – an American, Lane, and a New Zealand literary critic, Christina. The relationship between the two women is obscure: perhaps they are lovers, perhaps friends. After the accident, Lane checks her face for damage in one of the wing mirrors that was knocked off as the car somersaulted. It is a moment of great sangfroid and self-regard. With her red lips and clothing, the American is set up as a femme fatale. She is also callous: she abandons her badly injured friend and takes over her assignment to interview a Booker Prize winner. Christina had been bemoaning the lack of evil in New Zealand's benign countryside; Lane seems likely to rectify that.

Yet this is not a film that relies on such obvious delineations. Lane may be one of the more vivid characters in New Zealand cinema – first infatuating the Booker Prize-winning writer's daughter Angela, and then, via a haircut and a strange poi dance, seducing the writer himself – but *Crush* is not a film noir, and Lane is not a one-note femme. At times she is remorseful about her actions after the crash and her capricious treatment of Angela. At other times she is patronising and monstrous. The swing of her psyche from manipulative to vulnerable can be read as coping with shock or guilt, or disguising massive insecurities.

Crush
1992 / Feature / 91 mins

DIRECTOR / **Alison Maclean**
PRODUCER / **Bridget Ikin**
SCREENPLAY / **Alison Maclean, Anne Kennedy**
PRODUCTION COMPANY / **Hibiscus Films**

Unfortunately, a train of revenge is already rolling. The scorned Angela begins to visit brain-damaged Christina in hospital, poisoning her healing memory against Lane, and the movie shifts – not entirely convincingly – from a psychological drama to a disquieting thriller. Nevertheless, the ending is full of tension, and the scene where Christina arrives to stay the weekend at the writer's lakeside bach is deliciously creepy.

Cinematographer Dion Beebe gives the world a look of moist oppressiveness, finding the surreal and kitsch in Rotorua's tourist heart; the mud pools (and angular score by Jean-Paul Sartre Experience) are metaphors for the emotions bubbling below the surface.

In such a complex character study the acting must be of the highest order and it is. Donogh Rees and newcomer Caitlin Bossley lose nothing to future Oscar winner Marcia Gay Harden. While the movie is carried by Harden's compelling and nuanced performance, Bossley is entirely convincing as the smitten teen who copes with rejection through spite. Rees' work as a malevolent and unpredictable victim of head trauma is especially good. Why she is not a global star on the back of this performance is a mystery.

Like most of Alison Maclean's films, *Crush* is both erotic and confrontational. With its subject matter of obsession, loss of identity, disloyalty, manipulation, seduction, jealousy, self-deception and other deep human flaws, this menacing movie fits neatly into Sam Neill's description of New Zealand film as the cinema of unease.

A Death In The Family

THIS GROUND-BREAKING TELEVISION DRAMA, broadcast a year after homosexuality was legalised in New Zealand, was the first film anywhere in the world to deal directly with the experience of gay men and the AIDS epidemic. *An Early Frost*, an American movie that had come out the year before, had focussed on the victim's parents.

Andy, given three days to live, returns from Australia to a Grey Lynn villa to die. With his rural god-fearing family barely able to overcome their homophobia, his gay friends gather around to provide the support he needs. Emotions are mixed. There is fear, grief and anger – but also joie de vivre, laughter and the possibility of new love.

Most of the action is observed and commented on by Matt (Nigel Harbrow). Nervously meeting the dying man for the first time, he is surprised when Andy, listening to a Walkman, holds up his hand. 'Ranfurly Shield,' he whispers by way of explanation.

This kind of surprising detail raises *A Death In The Family* above mawkishness. Andy, even in extremis, is a rounded human being. He glares, rages and laughs. He smiles as his friends hold him in the shower and wash his body. He also memorably whispers, 'What a shit way to die.'

Inspired by the paintings of Caravaggio, Wells and Main create handsome tableaux. In one interesting sequence, Andy's death rattle plays over a time-lapse view of the villa. While the night's television programmes roll furiously on, Andy's breath catches in real time. After Andy dies, the camera sweeps several times past his bedroom window; at each pass the room is slowly stripped, until finally it is empty.

This is a mannered work – the eulogies directed straight to camera are particularly theatrical – but it is also a deeply emotional one. In spite of the short running time, the strong performances from the ensemble cast, especially Simon Prast, Elizabeth McRae and Jon Brazier, populate this house of grief with vividly real characters. This is not accidental: Main and Wells had experienced the death of a friend from AIDS the year before, and the film was shot on location in the house where he died.

A Death In The Family
1986 / Feature / 47 mins

DIRECTORS / **Stewart Main, Peter Wells**
PRODUCER / **James Wallace**
SCREENPLAY / **Peter Wells**
PRODUCTION COMPANY / **James Wallace Productions**

The Departure Of The Second Contingent For The Boer War

THE MOST REMARKABLE THING about this 45-second film is that it exists at all. It was made only five years after the Lumière Brothers had shown the first ever films – *Workers Leaving The Lumière Factory* and *Arrival Of A Train At La Ciotat Station* – to an excitable Paris audience in 1895. In October 1896, films of similarly laconic slices of life were shown in Auckland, and the audience cheered the moving figures in street scenes.

Alfred Whitehouse, a vaudevillean, was the first to import a Kinematograph camera to New Zealand. He proceeded to make ten films. The first showed the opening of the Auckland Industrial and Mining Exhibition. Several others depicted a waka regatta on the Waikato River at Ngaruawahia. In 1900 he filmed a parade of mounted cavalry at Wellington's Newtown Park, just before men and horses sailed to the South African conflict. All these works were thought to be lost.

In 1993 a fragile nitrate film was deposited with the New Zealand Film Archive. The images were clearly old and barely identifiable. The film stock was as brittle as eggshells and potentially unprintable. It was fume-treated to make it supple, then painstakingly repaired. Finally it was sent to Bologna in Italy, where a print was made off the nitrate. The repair work had taken 160 hours.

The print was examined by military historians, who agreed it was Whitehouse's lost film of the Second Contingent. The thrill watching this earliest surviving fragment of New Zealand film is probably the same as that felt by the Lumière brothers' first audience. You want to cheer the proud cavalrymen, wave at the crowd gathered beneath Mount Victoria's pines, and berate the boy who, in boater and starched collar, ambles in callow wonder in front of the camera. He stares back at us from 110 years ago.

The Departure Of The Second Contingent For The Boer War
1900 / Short / 45 seconds

DIRECTOR / PRODUCER
Alfred Whitehouse

Derek

AT A DINNER PARTY IN AUCKLAND in the early 1970s, a Shakespearean actor met an Australian geology student, and the New Zealand film industry would never be the same again. After a few drinks Ian Mune and Roger Donaldson decided to work together. The result was a short television movie about a disgruntled bureaucrat. If Mune and Donaldson were key members of New Zealand cinema's new wave, it is fair to call their telemovie, *Derek*, the shift in the seabed that started the waters moving.

Derek was filmed over a weekend at an office in downtown Auckland, with Mune in the title role of a lecherous misanthrope creating havoc on his last day at work, having recently been sacked. His sabotage of his office is a landmark in New Zealand comic acting, and the party that follows the close of business, including the first representation of binge-drinking on-screen in New Zealand, conversations in urinals and illicit sex, caused an uproar as the censor's boundaries were tested. The ending in which a drunk Derek returns to his suburban home, fractious wife and mid-life crisis is brilliantly tragicomic.

Mune and Donaldson picked up a Feltex Award for their efforts – 'We got a piece of carpet to prove it was the best film in New Zealand that year,' Donaldson remarked – and the pair next produced a series called *Winners And Losers*, which adapted numerous famous local short stories for television.

Their mighty collaboration finally spawned the landmark film *Sleeping Dogs*. Donaldson went on to become New Zealand's most successful export to Hollywood, while Mune remained at home, triumphing as an actor, screenwriter and director. Imagining cinema in New Zealand without these two and the monuments they have created is like imagining the Desert Road without Mounts Tongariro and Ngauruhoe.

Derek
1974 Feature 44 mins

DIRECTORS / SCREENPLAY
Roger Donaldson, David Mitchell, Ian Mune

PRODUCERS **Roger Donaldson, Ian Mune**

PRODUCTION COMPANY
Aardvark Films

Desperate Remedies

AN EXPLOSION OF HIGH MELODRAMA and even higher camp, *Desperate Remedies* channels Douglas Sirk, Emeric Pressburger, Rainer Werner Fassbinder and *The Magnificent Ambersons*, and adds gabardine, lace, sex and vials of opium.

Directors Peter Wells and Stewart Main had an almost pioneering attitude to the film's visuals, principally because of budget. As an antipodean Merchant Ivory production was not possible, with designer Michael Kane they embraced the garish and the gothic. An artificial world was created in a dockside storage shed. Special effects were improvised; on one notable occasion a headlong journey on a horse and dray was filmed with the use of reins, a fan, wobbly cartons, yards of scarlet fabric and a lot of acting.

Desperate Remedies has an unabashedly histrionic plot. Dorothea (Jennifer Ward-Lealand) is a Draper of Distinction in the colonial settlement of Hope, a quagmire of promiscuity and vice. Spying handsome new immigrant Lawrence (Kevin Smith), she sees him as a way to neutralise dastardly Fraser (Cliff Curtis), who… Well, the plot is an exercise in game theory, everyone trying to conceal their intentions and feelings in order to manipulate events. There are dark secrets, unrequited love, blackmail, drugs, political corruption and murder.

While not always engaging – the action is really only a coathanger on which to drape sumptuous costumes – the film is highly entertaining. The dialogue parodies the golden age of Hollywood, and witty lines crackle like fireworks. The performances are excellent, if never subtle: there are winks, sneers, smirks, pouts and long, lingering glances, as well as a giddy amount of male nudity.

Desperate Remedies
1993 Feature 92 mins

DIRECTORS SCREENPLAY
Stewart Main, Peter Wells
PRODUCER **James Wallace**
PRODUCTION COMPANY
James Wallace Productions

Fortunately, the opulence of the set design and Peter Scholes' operatic score hold your interest long after the plot has become a victim of its considerable excesses.

Drum/Sing

DRUM/SING IS THE FIRST of two collaborations between the innovative percussion group From Scratch and the film director Gregor Nicholas. While not as overtly political as the second, *Pacific 3-2-1-Zero*, an anti-nuclear film whose haunting chant of the names of damaged atolls decries testing in the South Pacific, *Drum/Sing* is a remarkable melding of music, performance and image. It is a sign of its success that the Museum of Modern Art in New York acquired a copy for its circulating film collection.

In the green room Phil Dadson stands on his head and we see the world from his perspective – inverted and slowed. The other musicians, Don McGlashan and Wayne Laird, limber up with hypnotic flexercises. In a flash the performance begins with the clapping and stomping of sandshoes, the plucking of a string on the floor, and singing. Then, in an explosion of sound and light, the musicians gravitate to their percussion stations – four-tier combinations of PVC slap pipes, tuned-tongue bells and bamboos, and roto tom drums.

In the first movement, Gregor Nicholas embraces the frenetic rhythms with fluid camera movements and editing: the camera swoops among the trio, cutting from one performer to another as the rhythm demands, and playing over the architecture of the instruments. In the second, he switches to intimate mood, examining the faces of the top-lit musicians and invoking a sense of conspiracy.

Drum/Sing

Pacific 3-2-1-Zero

Drum/Sing
1985 / Short / 22 mins

DIRECTOR / PRODUCER / Gregor Nicholas
CONCEPT / Phil Dadson, Gregor Nicholas

Drum/Sing was not Nicholas's first experiment with music and movement on film: *BodySpeak* had captured a trio of elaborate dances, while *Mouth Music* had presented an argument between a couple in music rather than words.

The End Of The Golden Weather

FROM ITS BEAUTIFUL SUN-CARESSED opening shot, *The End Of The Golden Weather* is a warm summer idyll set in the sand and lapping waters of the Hauraki Gulf. This is the reverie of a boy on the doorstep of adolescence, enjoying the last rays of childhood magic and imagination. The end of the golden weather is not only the time when the sun's rays begin to lose their heat, but the moment in a child's life when the magic dissipates and unromantic realities crowd in.

Geoff Crome, almost thirteen, dreams of becoming a famous writer. He has vivid fantasies, seeing the ramparts of a castle on the headlands and Herne the Hunter beneath the pohutukawa. He envisages himself exploring a subcontinental jungle in a pith helmet. Anything seems possible.

He befriends Firpo, a likeable, mentally impaired young man, played with thrilling exuberance by Stephen Papps (*Braindead, The Waiting Room*) in an award-winning performance. In 1930s Takapuna the friendship runs up against a climate of conformity and respectability, and when Firpo is cruelly mocked by the beach's young men Geoff tries to protect him from humiliation.

It took Ian Mune a decade and a half to realise his vision of turning Bruce Mason's solo stage play cum memoir into a film. At times the production seems to wear every minute of those fifteen years, feeling over-thought and overwrought. Generally, though, Mune

The End Of The Golden Weather
1991 / Feature / 103 mins

DIRECTOR / Ian Mune
PRODUCERS / Christina Milligan, Ian Mune
SCREENPLAY / Ian Mune, Bruce Mason
PRODUCTION COMPANY / South Pacific Pictures

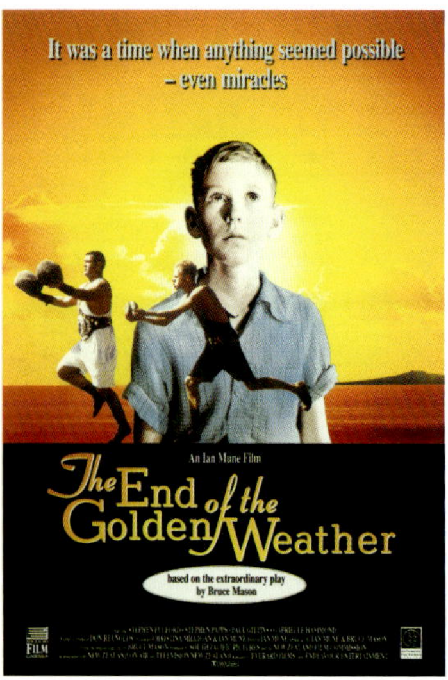

gets the tone just right. The Christmas party hosted by Geoff's parents, the Cromes, has the perfect mix of wonder and world-weariness: the adults drink, the children stage a chaotic play, and Father Christmas seduces Mrs Crome. At the climactic race scene on the beach, Firpo's skinny limbs fuel Geoff's belief that miracles can happen: the short sprint is beautifully filmed.

Stephen Fulford is excellent as Geoff. Also noteworthy are Paul Gittens as his father and David Taylor as his young brother. However, the downbeat ending of this film, in which Geoff marches off to the next stage of his life in a new school uniform, disconcerted audiences overseas. *The End Of The Golden Weather* remains a small domestic treasure.

The Feathers Of Peace

MORIORI, the indigenous people of the Chatham Islands, are believed to have arrived from their ancestral homeland in the early 1500s. After the second of their two migrations, fighting broke out, leading a high-ranking chief, Nunuku-whenua, to declare that Moriori were not to take up arms against other human beings. Feathers woven into the men's beards indicated their commitment to peace. This led to relatively peaceful European settlement, but tragically in 1835, when Maori tribes arrived from New Zealand on a mission of conquest – assisted, both actively and through acquiescence by the European settlers – genocide occurred. *The Feathers Of Peace* tells this story.

The film was a brave, controversial and uncompromising project: no less would have been expected of its Maori director, Barry Barclay (*The Neglected Miracle*, *Ngati*). Taking as his material historian Michael King's book *Moriori: A People Rediscovered*, Barclay exposes one of the grubbier secrets of the colonial era.

When Ngati Mutunga and Ngati Tama arrive in the Chathams they are seasick and dehydrated. Moriori care for them, but when the Maori recover they kill and enslave their hosts. Europeans living on the islands allow the murders to occur, and the pacifist Moriori effectively collude in their own destruction by steadfastly obeying Nunuku's Law.

Barclay dramatises these historical events in an unusual way.

Various incidents are shown with jumps and flaws, emulating archival footage. Interviews are conducted with actors playing the actual participants – William Broughton, captain of HMS *Chatham*, Moriori chiefs, European settlers and, most sadly, a Moriori woman, Waiteka – as if the events were news in the present day. Much of the dialogue is taken from written accounts, including court transcripts of the 1870 Land Court, where ninety-seven percent of Chatham Islands land was awarded to the invaders.

The Feathers Of Peace
2000 / Documentary / 88 mins

DIRECTOR / SCREENPLAY
Barry Barclay
EXECUTIVE PRODUCER
Don Selwyn
PRODUCER Ruth Kaupua
PRODUCTION COMPANY
He Taonga Films

This device, based on the quasi-newsreel idea pioneered by English director Peter Watkins in his 1964 film *Culloden*, initially seems hokey, but it allows the humanity of the victims of the extermination to be demonstrated in a way that could not have been achieved using archival stills. (It also has the effect of making the viewer question the veracity of current affairs interviews.)

There are stellar performances from Star Gossage as Waiteka, and Alan de Malmanche, Sonny Kirikiri, Calvin Tuteao and John Callen, among others. The film's four sections, covering eighty years of Chathams history, are divided by beautiful images of the islands, which are known to the Moriori as Rekohu – misty sky.

This innovative and confrontational film received the tribute of a limited commercial release, placing it alongside *Patu!*, *Kaikohe Demolition* and *War Stories Our Mothers Never Told Us* as one of New Zealand's best documentaries to date.

Flying Fox In A Freedom Tree

FROM THE OPENING CREDITS – shouted in Samoan over Polynesian drums – it is clear this is no ordinary feature film. Faifua Amiga, as Pepe, addresses the camera directly: terminally ill in hospital with tuberculosis, he is determined to tell his life story, one of frustration at cultural change in the South Pacific.

As he passes through his teenage years Pepe rejects the colonial values of Christianity and avarice embraced by his father in favour of the traditional ways of his village. However, when he realises these old ways are impossible to sustain he joins a street gang of outsiders, which includes a half-caste dwarf, Tangata – the flying fox of the title. After a church is burnt and Pepe makes a grandiloquent confession in court, he is sent to prison.

Based on an Albert Wendt story and set and filmed entirely in Western Samoa, this is an exceptionally ambitious first (and so far only) feature for Martyn Sanderson. The mélange of styles on display include a hallucinatory dream sequence on a lava field, a surreal fantasy of Pepe as an ancient god, naturalistic scenes at Apia's bus station and markets, and riotous action as Pepe and Tangata rip off a palagi at a nightclub.

At times the project seems amateurish: many in the cast and crew were having their first experience working in film. At other times the exuberance of the lead actors overrides any technical flaws. Amiga is outstanding, displaying the physicality and wit that marked his performances in *Kingpin* and *Mark II*, and poet and playwright Richard von Sturmer is magnetic as Tangata.

The film vividly evokes life in Samoa. Allen Guilford's lush cinematography lends a serenity to village scenes with an elderly chief, Toasa, that contrasts with the chaos and grubbiness of Apia's bars and streets. The intensity of saturated colour images lends a bright veneer to this bleak and powerful story of alienation.

Flying Fox In A Freedom Tree
1989 Feature 92 mins

DIRECTOR SCREENPLAY **Martyn Sanderson**
PRODUCER **Grahame McLean**
PRODUCTION COMPANY **Grahame McLean Associates**

Footage

NIKI CARO LIKES A CHALLENGE. Her first feature, *Memory And Desire*, focussed on Japanese culture, her second, *Whale Rider*, on Maori tradition, and her third, *North Country*, on a mining community near the United States' 49th Parallel. Before all this, however, Caro made a documentary. Its punning title is *Footage*, and it is a brilliant and stylised examination of shoes and their wearers.

Caro examines the history of various shoes – the bitch pump, the stiletto, the brothel-creeper, the knee-length boot and the 'democratic' trainer – in short, poetic vignettes. She interviews a forensic psychologist, cobblers, a fetishist, a tap-dancing teacher and a cross-dresser. She cuts in re-creations of historic events and shots from the field – a transgender woman's first encounters as a cross-dressing man are re-enacted, and a dominatrix session shown as it happens.

Caro's interest in strong characters, evident in her fiction films, is obvious. The horrors and history of, and rationale for, foot-binding in Chinese culture are examined by a university expert, Manying Ip, but it is Ip's personal experience of her grandmother's bound feet that is the most emotionally compelling. This is juxtaposed with stories from a dancer, Kerry-Anne Gilberd, about the extreme pain suffered by ballerinas.

The interviews are spliced with interpolations from Murray McNair, an articulate, witty podiatrist who sounds born for the stage with his anecdotes, classical quotes and oh so resonant voice. Caro's stylish interview sets, replete with chequerboard flooring and giant high-heeled shoe, are enhanced by judicious props and dramatic colour. The effect is quite hallucinatory. This is documentary, but the film-maker is pushing hard at its confines.

The real success of the film, though, is in the writing, Ballet shoes are, Caro suggests, 'pink-satin torture chambers'. Mules suggest 'virtue lost or about to be, without regret'. Platform shoes are where 'judgement was overridden by enthusiasm: individual expression clashed with disciplined design and came out victorious.'

Aptly, this highly original documentary was selected for the Venice Film Festival: Venice is the home of the platform shoe.

Footage
1996 / Documentary / 46 mins

DIRECTOR / SCREENPLAY / Niki Caro
PRODUCER / Owen Hughes
PRODUCTION COMPANY / Frame Up Films

Forgotten Silver

IT IS IMPOSSIBLE to discuss *Forgotten Silver* without issuing a spoiler alert. If you haven't seen the film and have no idea of its subject matter, put down this book and go see it. We'll meet again later.

When *Forgotten Silver* was first broadcast on New Zealand television it was a sensation. Many people were moved by the well-constructed historical documentary about our own Colin McKenzie, who filmed pioneer aviator Richard Pearse flying before the Wright Brothers, made the first ever 'talkie' (which failed at the box office because the actors were speaking Chinese), and pioneered colour film – although curious topless Tahitian women wandered into shot, resulting in McKenzie's arrest for indecency. This was number-eight-wire stuff, an imaginative lad from South Canterbury who invented a bike camera and experimented with making film from stripped flax and egg albumen.

Appearances by Leonard Maltin, Harvey Weinstein, John O'Shea and Peter Jackson confirmed that a great New Zealand artist had been rediscovered. So why do McKenzie's *Salome* or *Beloved Waters* not appear in this book? Largely because they were never made: *Forgotten Silver* was a brilliant hoax.

Jackson and co-director Costa Botes get the tone just right, consistently hinting at the truth without ever revealing it. There are clues throughout that the film is a spoof: a film researcher is called

Alexandra Nevsky; judges in court watch indecent footage over and over; Peter Jackson stumbles through thick bush. And I did notice that Colin McKenzie bore a strong resemblance to Tom from my local music store.

But while, viewed soberly, the plot may strain credibility, such is the quality and assurance of the documentary that intoxication sets in and disbelief is suspended. We want to believe in Colin McKenzie, his talent, his achievements and his frustrated ambition.

Jackson and Botes are film geeks. D.W. Griffith and the Lumière brothers are referenced, as are Rudall Hayward, Sergei Eisenstein, *The Lost Weekend* and *Citizen Kane*. The film also has a tilt at the infamous Rodney King video and *The Godfather*. The most fun seems to have been had making the lengthy excerpt from *Salome* – including ageing the film stock and perfecting the feel of silent movies.

Forgotten Silver
1995 / Feature / 56 mins

DIRECTORS / SCREENPLAY
Peter Jackson, Costa Botes
PRODUCER / Sue Rogers
PRODUCTION COMPANY
WingNut Films

The first television airing of *Forgotten Silver* was accompanied by an article in the *Listener* that gave no hint of the film's inauthenticity. The audience was completely taken in. The ensuing controversy, including a measure of public outrage, was similar to other moments when fiction has been presented as fact, including Orson Welles' radio play *The War Of The Worlds*, the *Brass Eye* television series and the films *Cannibal Holocaust* and *Borat*.

Why did we New Zealanders let the wool be pulled over our eyes? Perhaps it was because of the national myth that as a nation we punch above our weight, and can produce innovators such as Colin McKenzie. We have. One of them is called Peter Jackson.

Fracture

FRACTURE WAS RELEASED within months of *In My Father's Den* and dwarfed by the latter film's quality and assurance. Comparisons were readily made. Both films were adaptations of novels by the great New Zealand storyteller Maurice Gee and both dealt with the disaster zone of an 'ordinary' family. But while *Fracture*, adapted from Gee's *Crime Story*, may not reach the heights of *In My Father's Den*, it does not deserve to be forgotten. Every cent spent on the film is visible in its high production values and stellar cast, which includes Michael Hurst, Jennifer Ward-Lealand, Cliff Curtis, Nancy Brunning, Miranda Harcourt, Julian Arahanga, Alicia Fulford-Wierzbicki, Liddy Holloway, Sophia Hawthorne, Alistair Browning, Jed Brophy, Rawiri Paratene and Tim Lee. The best acting, however, comes from Wellington city, which quietly shimmers in every exterior shot.

Like the best Maurice Gee stories, the narrative initially seems frayed. Two families, the Rossers and the Peets, encounter each other briefly at the top of some stairs during an interrupted burglary, but the impact of their meeting will sorely test paternal and maternal bonds within these families. The novel's stamp is obvious in the potent dialogue and the inexorable way in which the threads of the narrative come together, often with unpredicted consequences.

Director Larry Parr's great skill is to have created so many convincing characters, most notably Leanne Rosser (Kate Elliot),

Fracture
2004 Feature 99 mins
DIRECTOR / SCREENPLAY
Larry Parr
PRODUCER Charlie McClellan
PRODUCTION COMPANY
Kahukura Productions

a solo mother rejected by her Christian mother, and Howard Peet (John Noble), a patriarch who bemoans the way his two children have turned out. Kate Elliot (*The Locals, Toy Love*) displays both feistiness and elfin fragility as she nurses her brother through his mental disintegration. Australian Noble (*Return Of The King, The Nostradamus Kid*), whether icily confronting his ex-wife (Liddy Holloway) or comforting his suicidal son, is both brusque and magnetic.

Fracture proved a prescient title for this film. Mismanagement of funds at post-production stage caused its production company to collapse, leaving debt and financial debris. *Fracture*, however, is a better film than its troubled upbringing would suggest.

Free Radicals

LEN LYE'S TOWERING KINETIC STRUCTURES *Wind Wand* and *Water Whirler* dominate the New Plymouth and Wellington waterfronts respectively. There is no less grandeur and art in the small scratch drawn on to celluloid with a Native American spear-head and antique dental equipment that is Lye's film *Free Radicals*. While the animation was created on a 16-millimetre 'canvas', when it is projected on to a big screen with light searing brightly through the markings it has the size and beauty of Lye's great metal sculptures.

The jagged lightning pirouettes and writhes to the sound of the Bagirmi tribe of Chad, appropriately a chant to the god of thunder. The letters of the title sequence leap in time to the drums. When singing begins on the field tape, vertical lines first sway, then seem to melt back into the blackness of the unscratched film. Shapes and tangled images combine, sometimes like graffiti, at other times like relief maps, fretboards, asterisks or brushstrokes. Occasionally a single scratch will pivot and spin, as if the void of the frame is three-dimensional space, before it fractures into tiny shards.

Almost impossibly minimalist, *Free Radicals* is also one of the most bewitching of films. Many of the individual frames are art-works in themselves, although to take a single frame is to negate the hallucinogenic quality of the movement.

Free Radicals
1958 / Short / 4 mins
DIRECTOR / PRODUCER / CONCEPT
Len Lye

The brevity of this film does not reflect the effort that went into creating it: the four minutes took Lye all of eight months to complete. He scratched in what he called a rhythmic trance, digging through the black emulsion but being careful not to tear the film, and often scratching by instinct as he was unable to see the separate frames distinctly. He named his miniature masterpiece after the fundamental particles in chemical reactions: their instability matched the kinesthesia he had created.

The Frog, The Dog And The Devil

AT THE 1986 ACADEMY AWARDS, New Zealand director Bob Stenhouse was seated next to Californian John Lasseter (*Toy Story*, *Cars*). Both were nominated for Best Short Animated Film, Lasseter for his computer-animated short *Luxo Jr.* and Stenhouse for *The Frog, The Dog And The Devil.* Both assumed the other would win. The Oscar went to a Belgian film-maker. Nonetheless, the innovativeness of Stenhouse's film, with its lustrous colour and vibrant animation, is still lauded in animation circles: in 2000 *The Frog, The Dog And The Devil* was voted one of eighty-four jewels of the twentieth century at France's Annecy International Animation Festival.

Stenhouse has continued to make charming animations, including *The Orchard*, a beguiling story about a tsunami, inspired by a Japanese folk tale, and *Fisherboy* and *Incredible Creature* from stories by the children's writer Joy Cowley.

The Frog, The Dog And The Devil is based on 'The Devil's Daughter', a ballad by Ernie Slow. Slow was an itinerant farmhand and shearer in the South Island's Mackenzie Country, and this is a rollicking temperance yarn with some macabre humour. A swagman finesses a bottle of whisky from a saloon but pays dearly: as the demon drink starts having an influence he is possessed by the 'devil in the glass', which takes him and his dog on a terrifying night ride as thunderheads brew and lightning flashes. The man finally arrives back at the pub, needing a drink.

The Frog, The Dog And The Devil
1986 / Short / 7 mins

DIRECTOR / SCREENPLAY / **Bob Stenhouse**

PRODUCERS / **Hugh MacDonald, Martin Townsend**

PRODUCTION COMPANY / **New Zealand National Film Unit**

Visually, the film is breathtaking. The glowing effect was laboriously achieved by Stenhouse, who described it as the animation equivalent of printing the Gutenberg Bible.

First, the top picture was re-exposed and underlit through various devices, such as opal glass, to spread the light and impose a lantern glow or other desired effect. To add a further effect, the shutter was then closed and the film rewound. Some 250 pieces of artwork were passed 3000 times; one sequence was exposed almost thirty times. In America, Stenhouse was asked if he were worried his innovative technique would be stolen. No, he replied, no one would be stupid or masochistic enough to follow it.

A Game With No Rules

IF THERE IS AN ANTIPODEAN HEIR to Alfred Hitchcock, it is Scott Reynolds. Reynolds' 1998 feature film *The Ugly* may be more graphic and supernatural than anything Hitchcock made, but its architecture of suspense is superb. A scene in which street lights intermittently illuminate the leather upholstery of the killer's classic car is worthy of the master himself: we know what the back seat contains, but are still shocked when it is finally revealed.

Reynolds' short *A Game With No Rules* starts with opening credits that could have been designed by Hitchcock's collaborator, Saul Bass, then kicks off a nicely layered plot that has a little *Rope*,

A Game With No Rules
1994 / Short / 16 mins

DIRECTOR / SCREENPLAY /
Scott Reynolds
PRODUCER / Jonathan Dowling
PRODUCTION COMPANY /
Zee Films

a touch of *Strangers On A Train* and a dram of *Psycho*. In a luridly lit bar, Kane (Marton Csokas) approaches Vera, a pretty young woman (Danielle Cormack), with a bold suggestion: murder for profit. He is unhappily married to Lauren (Jennifer Ward-Lealand), a bisexual heiress. The avaricious Vera agrees to be used as bait.

What follows is an exercise in style, saluting noir films with back projection, femmes fatales, retro costuming, and occasional homage to Quentin Tarantino. The film's bold lighting and camerawork and the stylised performances from the three leads lend the entire quarter of an hour a deliberate, glorious artificiality. It is topped off with a graphically realised and surprising twist.

Gone Up North For A While

NOT MANY FILMS CAN CLAIM to have affected real social change, but New Zealand has at least two. *Indictment!* (1950) was an incendiary work about the squalor in which elderly were living in Auckland's Freemans Bay. Commissioned by cinema mogul Robert Kerridge, it was shown throughout his theatres to raise consciousness about elder neglect, and funds for the City Mission.

Gone Up North For A While, produced in 1972 by the National Film Unit, had an even more direct effect. Broadcast on the lone television channel, this story of an unmarried teenager having a baby and trying to exist in a vacuum of financial and emotional support attracted a large audience and influenced public opinion at a time when a bill establishing a benefit for unwed mothers was being introduced to parliament.

The film opens with Jane giving her details to a nurse. She pauses when asked about 'marital status'; her action in sticking chewing gum under the lid of a desk signals that this is a young girl. As she walks through the hospital corridors to the birthing room, her mind flashes back to the baby's conception and her subsequent rejection by her boyfriend, employer, institutions, friends and parents.

Director Paul Maunder was influenced by the socio-realist films of Ken Loach. Much of the film's dialogue was improvised: Denise Maunder as the young mother and Paul Holmes as her fleeting beau are particularly impressive. But European influences

Gone Up North For A While
1972 / Feature / 39 mins

DIRECTOR / SCREENPLAY / Paul Maunder
PRODUCER / Ronald Bowie
PRODUCTION COMPANY / New Zealand National Film Unit

also shine through – non-linear narrative, hand-held camera and jump cuts.

Maunder was one of a quintet of film-makers who brought the French new wave to New Zealand cinema. Although he worked in different styles, circumstances and locations to Geoff Steven, Geoff Murphy, Roger Donaldson and Tony Williams, his impact cannot be overestimated. With his strong political focus, he often grasped awkward subjects. Another of his televised films, *One Of Those People That Live In The World* (1974), dealt with schizophrenia, while *Sons For The Return Home* (1979) was the first feature film to examine the experience of Pacific Islanders living in New Zealand.

Goodbye Pork Pie

GOODBYE PORK PIE HAS A STRANGE HOLD over the New Zealand psyche: its yellow Mini has become as iconic as buzzy bee, L&P and stubbies. The film was the first local feature to be an unqualified success at the box office, and when it was first shown on television half of the adult population tuned in. Its star Kelly Johnson, now a criminal lawyer in Northland, still gets regaled with calls of 'Blondini!' when meeting clients at prisons.

Essentially the longest car chase ever filmed, *Goodbye Pork Pie* celebrates the friendship of blokes, hooning around in cars, and an anti-authoritarian spirit in the New Zealand temperament that is perhaps more mythical than real. The skeleton of a tale – a young delinquent commits an opportunistic petty crime, and an older man joins the getaway ride to Invercargill in order to repair his marriage – is given flesh by the quality of acting by the two leads, Johnson and Tony Barry. Johnson seems as though he could power a small South Island town with his manic energy.

Goodbye Pork Pie was inspired by a hitchhiking incident in which freelance film producer Chris Francis was picked up by a pair who sold bits of their rental car on their journey. When the story was related to director Geoff Murphy, he enlarged it into an anarchic road movie. Murphy had been in Blerta, Bruno Lawrence's travelling music troupe, and the movie channels the troupe's exuberance – not surprisingly as members Lawrence, Barry, Ian Watkin, Alun

Goodbye Pork Pie
1981 Feature 106 mins

DIRECTOR Geoff Murphy
PRODUCERS Geoff Murphy, Nigel Hutchinson
SCREENPLAY Geoff Murphy, Ian Mune
PRODUCTION COMPANY AMA Productions

Bollinger and their extended families were all key contributors.

The film is a celebration of inventiveness: it was filmed chronologically, ingenuity was required to overcome production hurdles, and many of the crew were learning on the job. Despite this, the impossible seems achieved in every second shot, many of which involve well-rendered stunts. One, in which a police car careers into a lake, was performed by the director himself. Particularly noteworthy is the slalom driving at Wellington Railway Station: with the mini packed with camera, cast and crew, handbrake turns were the only way to achieve the tight cornering. The nationwide filming was, in effect, a brilliant grassroots marketing campaign that engendered enthusiasm for the movie before it was even in the can.

From the title card onwards, much of the humour in *Goodbye Pork Pie* is indigenous, and thirty years on some has dated badly. The sexism and chauvinism seem from another age entirely. Equally, the narrative drive occasionally parks up and some of the scenes drag, and not in the road-race meaning of the word. Nevertheless, there is still power in many of the film's hilarious deadpan lines.

Haunting Douglas

OCCASIONALLY THERE IS A DOCUMENTARY SUBJECT so compelling that he or she outshines characters in fiction films and the actors who play them. An example is the arrogant, caustic, pretentious, witty, charming, cynical and hugely talented dancer and choreographer Douglas Wright.

Right from the opening sequence, in which Wright moves across a stage with a lit candle for a phallus, *Haunting Douglas* is in your face and, like its subject, uncompromising. Whether it's the bullying criticism Wright barks at dancers during rehearsals of his next work or the videoed encounters in which he questions the very process of making a documentary, some scenes are difficult to watch. At one point Wright directly confronts director Leanne Pooley, via her camera, accusing her of exploiting painful parts of his personal history. It becomes clear that this is a fragile arrangement, a quid pro quo: Wright is exposing the ghosts of past recklessness in order for his dance oeuvre to be seen again.

The film's most dazzling sequences are of Wright's work, in which his physical muscularity dominates. *Halo*, *Now is the Hour*, *Arc3*, *Gloria*, *Forever* and *Dead Dreams of Monochrome Men*, and archival footage of his performances with Limbs and the Paul Taylor Dance Company, with whom he danced in New York in the 1980s, would be enough to justify classing *Haunting Douglas* as an essential New Zealand film. However, the Faustian pact

Haunting Douglas
2003 / Documentary / 75 mins

DIRECTOR / SCREENPLAY / Leanne Pooley

PRODUCERS / Leanne Pooley, Shona McCullagh

PRODUCTION COMPANY / Spacific Films

with Pooley means that we also voyeuristically view a life in which luxuriant talent writhes in a pas de deux with self-destruction.

Wright's personal life is revealed through startlingly frank interviews with his lovers and collaborators, and the HIV-positive dancer himself reading passages from his autobiography and answering questions in intimate, soft-spoken interviews. When he describes the last time he danced before his illness began to diminish his extraordinary strength and stamina, his sorrow and pain are palpable.

At other times the mood is radically different: as the documentary is put together Wright sifts dismissively through old photos, argues with Pooley about getting a bad review, and sneers at a release form.

Technically and conceptually, arts documentaries don't come better than *Haunting Douglas.* Mythologising is avoided. Instead, its subject is shown as a full human being, resilient, creative and confrontational – burning with anger and inspiration even as he is haunted by a devastating illness.

Heavenly Creatures

WHEN IT WAS ANNOUNCED THAT as a follow-up to *Braindead* Peter Jackson was to direct a film version of the Parker-Hulme case, many people wondered if the murder scene would last several reels. However, Jackson shucked off his splatter mantle with this extraordinary study of a society – conservative, socially stratified Christchurch of the 1950s – and an obsessive friendship between two teenage girls that led to matricide.

The movie begins with a *Pictorial Parade* of the garden city and its 'more English than the English' ambience. Suddenly, the quiet is

Heavenly Creatures
1994 / Feature / 105 mins

DIRECTOR / **Peter Jackson**
PRODUCER / **James Booth**
SCREENPLAY / **Peter Jackson, Fran Walsh**
PRODUCTION COMPANY / **WingNut Films**

shattered by the screaming of two bloodied girls. The connection between these images provides the substance of the film.

Heavenly Creatures has excellent casting. The two leads – Kate Winslet, in her first movie role, and untrained Melanie Lynskey, found during a trawl of New Zealand secondary schools – not only look like the actual protagonists but conjure up an entirely believable intense friendship. From different social classes, the girls bond as outsiders with vivid, scary imaginations. The charismatic Juliet's affection for her awkward working-class school friend Pauline develops quickly: regularly abandoned by her emotionally distant parents, she craves a comrade.

The dangerous fantasy world the girls create contrasts with blunt realities. Juliet is sickly and her mother libidinous. Pauline has a clumsy first sexual encounter with a male boarder, and her mother frets about her 'unhealthy' friendship with Juliet. A lesbian relationship is suggested but not exploited.

Jackson proved here that he could direct people as well as puppets and latex. True, there is a little too much running and squealing from the girls, and the Borovnian fantasy scenes feel over-indulgent, but such criticisms are churlish. This is an intricately detailed movie, based on rigorous research. The murder scene, in which the girls exchange urgent looks to the accompaniment of Puccini's 'Humming Chorus' and then visit bloody horror on Pauline's mother, is one of the masterstrokes of New Zealand cinema.

I Want To Be Joan

HERE IS PROOF POSITIVE that cinema can be socially revolutionary. *I Want To Be Joan* was developed after the director, Stephanie Beth, was invited to the United Women's Conference in Christchurch in 1977. What was originally meant to be a filmic record of the conference became something greater – a documentary that gave voice to the women of the silent majority. The six women subjects hadn't spoken during the conference workshops, but Beth managed to coax them in front of her camera. This was a different way to find compelling interviewees, but it worked: there was honesty and power in their stories.

The revelations in *I Want To Be Joan* would not be considered explosive today since the downsides of marriage for many women have been widely canvassed – including in films such as *Irene 58* and *Rud's Wife* – but at the time they verged on the sensational. Some women talked of violence and abuse, others simply of lack of fulfillment in the traditional female roles of wife and mother. The hesitant confessions of Joan Lyes, a long-term psychiatric patient, provided the film's title: 'I tried to be supermum and that didn't work. Then I tried to be superwife and that didn't work either. So now I want to be just Joan.'

The opening shot of one of Christchurch's newly built suburbs magnifies the emptiness and bleakness of domestic life for many women. Interspersed with the interviews is a montage of photo-

I Want To Be Joan
1977 / Documentary / 32 mins

DIRECTOR / PRODUCER / WRITER Stephanie Beth

graphs, paintings by Robin White and Jan Zilstra, and a poem by Rachel McAlpine.

Stephanie Beth spent a year touring *I Want To Be Joan*, screening it more than a hundred times on borrowed projectors in village halls and homes, to women's community groups and schools. Its impact was considerable. Today, the film's simple truths and grassroots distribution place it in the vanguard of feminist film-making in New Zealand.

Illustrious Energy

THE BARE, BIG-SKIED BEAUTY of Central Otago has inspired Brian Turner, Janet Frame and the region's artist-in-residence Grahame Sydney, but the Ida and Nevis valleys have rarely been given such lustre as in Leon Narbey's *Illustrious Energy*.

Narbey is New Zealand's answer to great cinematographers such as Néstor Almendros and Haskell Wexler, and although Alan Locke was director of photography on this film, throughout you can feel Narbey's genius for the shot. As the lens lingers over clouds, sunsets, schist rock formations and tussocked hills, it seems possible to take out single frames and mount them.

The elegant plot follows Chinese immigrants of the late nineteenth century as they toil long hours on the Otago goldfields for a meagre glitter in the bottom of their pans – gold that will bring them closer to buying a return ticket to China and their families. The everyday rhythms of working the claims provide a counterpoint to the chaos, vice and violence in the township. The script, at times Zen-like in its simplicity, illuminates the disconnection of the miners from their homeland – they are as trapped as the pet cricket they keep. But lead character Chan's philosophy is fatalistic: 'Heaven is just the sky… I see the sky. I feel the earth. I walk in between like any man.'

The plot is more complex than the film's alternative title, *Dreams Of Home,* may suggest. It is not simply about a man's thwarted

Illustrious Energy
1988 / Feature / 96 mins

DIRECTOR / **Leon Narbey**
PRODUCERS / **Don Reynolds, Chris Hampson**
SCREENPLAY / **Leon Narby, Martin Edmond**
PRODUCTION COMPANY / **Mirage Entertainment**

desire to return to his wife and a child he has never seen: scenes with another migrant, Wong, show the possibilities offered by life in the colony if compromises are made and past lives foregone, and the opium Chan consumes is as much hedonism as escapism.

There is wooden acting from some minor characters, but not from lead actor Shaun Bao nor his love interest, played by Geeling Ng, who smokes up the screen in possibly the sexiest role in a New Zealand film to date. In a grace note, many of the extras are descendants of the original Chinese migrants.

35

In My Father's Den

BRAD MCGANN MADE ONLY ONE FEATURE FILM before his untimely death but it is a great film, and one that should be mentioned every time there is a discussion about the best New Zealand film of all time. Based on the Maurice Gee novel of the same name, the story follows Paul Prior, a renowned photojournalist, as he returns to his hometown for the first time in seventeen years. His father has recently died and his estate is being resolved.

Paul, moodily played by British actor Matthew Macfadyen, is a

man with too many stamps in his passport. He is emotionally and sexually jaded. When he meets Celia, an awkward, creative, intelligent teenager, played immaculately by Emily Barclay, he recognises something of himself in her. When Celia disappears, he becomes the centre of suspicion – the outsider who has picked at the frayed yarns of a close-knit society.

In My Father's Den
2004 / Feature / 122 mins

DIRECTOR / SCREENPLAY / **Brad McGann**
PRODUCERS / **Trevor Haysom, Dixie Linder**
PRODUCTION COMPANY / **THE Film/Little Bird**

There are some bold changes from the novel. Most successfully, the setting is transplanted to photogenic Central Otago. The warm and barren landscape that filled the frames of *50 Ways Of Saying Fabulous*, *Battletruck* and *Starlight Hotel* becomes, in the hands of cinematographer Stuart Dryburgh, close and claustrophobic.

In My Father's Den would not have been half as successful without McGann's superb screenplay, which convinced both Macfadyen and Dryburgh to join the project. The dialogue always seems right without being trite. Pithy lines ripple with barely suppressed anger in the scenes between Paul and his brother Andrew (a convincing Colin Moy). Secrets are exposed in a shocking dénouement that has the heady pace of a thriller.

It could be argued that *In My Father's Den* – dealing with psychological violence in the home (as well as repressed emotions and hidden schisms within a family, stifling puritanical Christianity, distrust of dreamers and intellectuals, and struggles against small-town mundanity) – is a pakeha *Once Were Warriors*. Whether the theory fits or not, this is an involving and revealing tour de force.

In Spring One Plants Alone

VINCENT WARD WAS A STUDENT OF PAINTING at Ilam School of Fine Arts when he discovered cinema. His first film, an assured adaption of Janet Frame's *State Of Siege* (and described by Frame herself as 'a beautiful poem'), was made when he was just out of his teens. His second, *In Spring One Plants Alone*, showed a remarkable commitment to the moving image – Ward spent two

years in the remote Urewera region living with a Tuhoe kuia, Puhi, and her schizophrenic son Niki.

In Spring One Plants Alone
1980 / Documentary
45 mins

DIRECTOR / PRODUCER / WRITER
Vincent Ward

The result is a different piece of cinema. This is an observational documentary: the audience is given no context, just a series of astoundingly aesthetic images photographed by Ward, Alun Bollinger and Leon Narbey. The camera concentrates on small details – Niki clicking his fingers or shielding his eyes, Puhi intoning continuous karakia as she subsists in the most basic conditions, her bent frame stooping over a coal range or collecting water. In this context, the scenes in town at the barber shop or buying ice blocks seem odd: we are suddenly propelled from an ancient fellahin existence into a gaudy modern world.

Some scenes are magical. In the opening sequence, a car journeys down a track in the dark of night, only to encounter Niki with its headlights. A horse appears out of the mist.

Other scenes are affecting. When Puhi talks directly to the camera about Niki's violence, her fear is palpable. In the final heartbreaking shot, we see her chopping wood as the camera pulls back to reveal Niki standing nearby with his back to her, staring at the suffocating lushness.

In Spring One Plants Alone was not widely seen. Although it had a limited cinema release, perversely Ward did not want it shown. Puhi had died that year and because of the deep affection he had developed for her, he sought to honour the memory of this fascinating and forbearing woman.

Infection

JAMES CUNNINGHAM ONCE DECLARED he had made three movies and never been behind a camera. This is because *Delf*, *Blinder* and *Infection* are all CGI – computer-generated imagery – animated shorts. Existing in the unseen world behind human–computer relations, the characters are Delfs – digitally engineered life forms: some run around playing tag before finding themselves in the wireframe world; others struggle with a belligerent operating system.

In *Infection* the Delf is a computer virus, launched by its creator

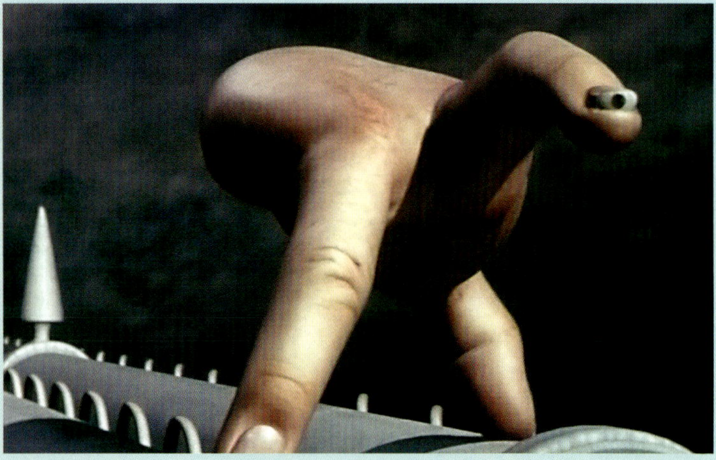

to wipe out a student loan. It takes the form of a hand with an eye on one of its fingers. The vigilant administrators are large eyeballs that crawl. When the virus is discovered, a platoon of hypodermic needles is released: cue a tribute to Jet Li and John Woo action films.

Infection
2000 / Short / 9 mins

DIRECTOR / SCREENPLAY / **James Cunningham**
PRODUCER / **Paul Swadel**
PRODUCTION COMPANY / **Supercollider Productions**

Infection is marvellously detailed, technically proficient and very funny. The fight scenes are vibrant – *Infection*'s digital hero may be New Zealand cinema's best exponent of martial acts. That Cunningham managed to imbue an animated hand with such emotion, including in an oddly poignant death scene, suggests why this short was nominated for a Palme d'Or at Cannes.

Jack Be Nimble

THE HORROR GENRE in New Zealand film has been beset by two things – most of the frighteners dip quickly towards incomprehensibility, and others are so derivative that tension is impaled by predictability. Nevertheless, there have been spectacular moments: some scenes in *The Ugly* are truly creepy; the short *French Doors* is nicely framed; *Pikowae* is haunting if opaque; *The Lost Tribe* is full of atmosphere, even if its plot is as misty as the fjords; *When Night Falls* is a well-made, if mechanical, thriller.

The pinnacle, however, is Garth Maxwell's *Jack Be Nimble*. The story follows Jack and Dora, separated out for adoption as children but connected psychically. Starting with their mother being battered by sheets on a clothesline as she mentally disintegrates, and curtains billowing in an art deco home, this film is visually dazzling. Many images – for example the blood of a slaughtered pig dissolving into a birthday cake, four vengeful sisters crowding into the cab of a truck, and Jack being whipped with barbed wire by his adoptive father – print themselves indelibly on the mind.

With so much cruelty on screen *Jack Be Nimble* is difficult to watch at times, but with a plot fuelled by parental irresponsibility, childhood trauma and their consequences, it does attempt a psychological depth that most horrors avoid. Although the narrative is wildly confused – the viewer occasionally needs Dora's psychic ability to divine what is going on – the film manages to sustain a pungent gothic atmosphere. The collection of images becomes hypnotic – spell-binding the viewer, just as Jack's strange light machine mesmerises his abusive foster family.

Jack Be Nimble
1993 Feature 93 mins

DIRECTOR / SCREENPLAY / Garth Maxwell
PRODUCERS / Jonathan Dowling, Kelly Rogers

The lead performances are top-drawer, and the enduring affection between the siblings believable and affecting. As Dora, Sarah Smuts-Kennedy fittingly balances melodrama and emotional complexity. Californian transgender actress Alexis Arquette, as the unhinged Jack, produces a performance of deep rage and a completely acceptable New Zealand accent, flattened vowels and all. Bruno Lawrence, playing Teddy in his last role in a New Zealand film before his death, is moody but somewhat wasted.

Kaikohe Demolition

NEW ZEALAND HAS BEEN DESCRIBED as the place old cars come to die. A lot of them die in Kaikohe. The Northland town achieved worldwide infamy when Santa got mugged there by some kids in the 1990s, but now the kids have grown up and joined the veterans in the Demolition Derby. Florian Habicht was inspired to make this film by derby king John Zielinksi and charismatic real-life characters such as Ben Haretuku, a bouncer who facilitates anger management courses. Habicht finds poetry in the damaged panels and stoved-in bumpers, and ballet in a Valiant's last drive.

There is a moment in *Kaikohe Demolition* where an attractive teenage girl is licking an ice cream. At first the shot seems gratuitous – until the cars race past and the girl puts up her hand to shield the ice cream from the mud flying off the churning wheels. Less subtle but no less funny is Zielinski adding to tyre tread with a chainsaw. It is just such hilarious and intricate observations that make *Kaikohe Demolition* a pleasure to watch.

Habicht is from Northland (he won best decorated bike at Paihia Primary School in 1985) and *Kaikohe Demolition* portrays life as it is lived in the far north, but the film has surreal moments, including an old man standing outside Ngawha Springs and just about any scene featuring the toothless Uncle Bimm. Touchingly, there is also a shot of Santa being merrily welcomed by a gaggle of young children, 'suggesting,' as one reviewer noted, 'that past differences

Kaikohe Demolition
2004 / Documentary /
55 mins

DIRECTOR / PRODUCER / WRITER /
Florian Habicht
PRODUCTION COMPANY /
Pictures for Anna

have been patched up.'

Habicht never patronises. He both understands and embraces the Northland psyche and knows the importance of retaining the integrity of your radiator. Without such empathy he would never have got such candour from his subjects, especially during their post-carnage soaks in hot pools. This is a warm muddy postcard from a rural, low-decile and predominantly Maori community.

Kingpin

MIKE WALKER'S COMMITMENT to showing the lives of disaffected, mainly Polynesian youth led to a trilogy films, all starring Mitch Manuel. *Kingi's Story* showed how the title character ended up in a police cell: the screenplay was constructed after a series of interviews with youth detainees. *Kingpin*, the second movie, deals with the next step – detention at a boys' training centre.

The three lead characters are introduced with a freeze frame as long lists of their convictions are typed on to the screen. Karl (Nicholas Rogers), the kingpin, uses his size and influence over sycophants to intimidate the other boys. Willie (Junior Amiga), the joker, resists with wit what he cannot with his small frame. The arrival at the centre of a 'real hard jube', Riki (Manuel), provides the narrative drive as the others try to divine where he will fit into the pecking order.

Willie sees Riki as a challenger to Karl's bullying, and a friendship develops. Then a series of disappointments – Willie's adolescent crush on one of the staff, Ms Eastwood (Judy McIntosh), is spurned, a letter to his father is returned to sender, his story about a girl he is seeing is shown to be fiction, Riki is injured in a forestry accident – leads to an escape attempt. Euphoric and brief, it ends with a shocking and spectacular car crash.

Some of *Kingpin*'s narrative devices are heavy-handed, and the resolution is melodramatically macho, but the film is perfectly pitched at its target teenage audience. From the arresting start, with institutional work boots either stomping a rhythm or moon-walking (break-dance champion Niu Satele), to the brawl that ends with the kingpin unconscious in a urinal, this is an engrossing ride.

The adult characters, who include fine supporting turns from Jim Moriarty, Kevin Wilson and Terence Cooper, avoid caricature: one of Walker's great skills is to render even minor characters believable, with their own vernacular and motivations. And the film offers no excuses: it is never suggested that even the most likeable kids do not deserve to be inmates. Some of the root causes are hinted at – Riki's father, played by Wi Kuki Kaa, is an alcoholic for example – but this is social realism, not agitprop.

Kingpin was filmed in the soulless rooms and common spaces of the Kohitere Boys' Training Centre, and many of the actors were

inmates. Manuel, the only one with acting experience, performs like a coiled spring, all potency and energy behind his broad smile. He had been incarcerated at Kohitere when discovered by Walker for *Kingi's Story*, and wrote the screenplay for *Kingpin* while in prison for armed robbery. The amateur status of the rest of the cast rarely shows. The star turn is the youngest actor, Faifua Amiga (*Flying Fox In A Freedom Tree*, *Variations On A Theme*), as stroppy, cheeky Willie, who shines with charm.

Kingpin
1985 Feature 89 mins

DIRECTOR **Mike Walker**
PRODUCERS **Gary Hannam, Mike Walker**
SCREENPLAY **Mike Walker, Mitch Manuel**
PRODUCTION COMPANY **Morrow Productions**

Kitchen Sink

IN THE LATE 1980s the Film Commission sponsored some 'bonsai epics' – small films with big ideas. *Kitchen Sink* by Alison Maclean (*Taunt, Talkback*) was one of them. This taut film starts with a nod to *Psycho* as water pours down a plughole (clockwise, of course), but then moves on to *King Kong, Un Chien Andalou, Repulsion, The Fly, Woman Of The Dunes* and, most especially, *Eraserhead.* It is, in other words, a complete *101: Introduction to Cinema* course.

Despite its title, the film is not a domestic drama, more a surreal horror romance. With its birth metaphors, abjection, feminist theory, Pygmalion and Galatea myths, and a schoolgirl selling mystery envelopes, it has everything – including the eponymous kitchen sink.

This near-silent movie tells its story almost exclusively in pictures. Theresa Healey (*Jubilee, Bread And Roses*) finds in her plumbing a tiny creature that swells into a hairy and inert man. She decides to civilise the apelike creature – shaving his body, clipping his eyebrows, and sharing a bed with him. But when he remains passive she shoves him in a bin liner.

Kitchen Sink exists in the demilitarised zone between the sexes, full of threat and the intoxication of danger. The style of the film, with its shadows, close-ups and mise en scène, owes much to the horror traditions: Healey often has her back to the creature and the climactic fight over a naked blade is straight from a slasher pic.

The film is not completely comfortable viewing: Stuart Dryburgh's black and white images, the sound design – in particular the amplified noise of a cut-throat razor scraping across the man's body – and the atmospheric metallic score by Headless Chickens are unsettling. The story oscillates from funny to frightening, with a healthy dose of eroticism and a dash of M.C. Escher.

Kitchen Sink
1989 Short 14 mins

DIRECTOR SCREENPLAY
Alison Maclean
PRODUCER **Bridget Ikin**
PRODUCTION COMPANY
Hibiscus Films

The Little Things

ONE THING THAT SHINES OUT of any survey of New Zealand film is the quality of child actors the country has produced. Every second film seems to unearth a new remarkable young talent, Oscar winner Anna Paquin and nominee Keisha Castle-Hughes being merely the most renowned. Melanie Lynskey, Greer Robson, Alicia Fulford-Wierzbicki, Stephen Fulford, Lee Mete-Kingi, Alexia Keogh, Hamish McFarlane, Fiona Kay and Emily Barclay have also carried feature films on their slim shoulders – a tribute to casting directors such as Liz Mullane and Diana Rowan.

It was Rowan who unearthed fourteen-year-old Norissa Taia and six-year-old Romain Waerea for *The Little Things*. George and Tama are two marginalised children existing in Whangarei's suburban blight. It is George's fourteenth birthday and she has been abandoned for the evening by her mother in favour of a romantic liaison. Her father is absent, and Tama, the young kid from next door, is a nuisance. George may be only on the cusp of adulthood but she already knows the harshness of an indigent life in a state housing ghetto. As she tells Tama: 'Life sucks. You should get used to it.'

George heads out to enjoy her birthday in other ways – shoplifting and vandalism – before returning home bored and despondent. Her invitation to Tama to share cake – and a clandestine bourbon and coke – is merely an attempt to dispel her loneliness, but the pride with which he accepts the offer is disarming. His makeshift birthday present and slapstick dancing puncture the tough veneer the teenager has been projecting. The little things are also those acts of aroha and empathy that really matter.

The Little Things
2004 Short 12 mins

DIRECTOR SCREENPLAY
Reina Webster
PRODUCER Catherine Fitzgerald
PRODUCTION COMPANY
Blueskin Films

The Little Things has similar subject matter to *Two Cars, One Night* and Reina Webster's direction is no less assured or gentle than Taika Waititi's. This beautiful, finely drawn film about unexpected generosity and kindness amid arid neglect is cinéma vérité at its most uplifting.

The Lord Of The Rings

THE ENORMOUS CRITICAL AND FINANCIAL SUCCESS of Peter Jackson's Rings trilogy took New Zealand film-making into a new sphere. The image of Jackson holding aloft the Oscar for best film for *The Return Of The King* is like an exclamation mark in its history.

Although the individual films won awards, *The Lord Of The Rings* was conceived as a single work and filmed at one time. It was then edited into three parts for annual release, just as J.R.R. Tolkien's original book had been rent into three because of budgetary and marketing constraints.

Only the most pedantic or unpatriotic would quibble with this being a 'New Zealand' film. Tolkien wrote the saga in England, using influences from German, Norse and other mythologies, but the film version has became so linked with the New Zealand landscape and so embraced by the population that Kiwis now claim their own quarter-acres of Middle-earth. The New Zealand countryside is, indeed, the real star of the film. The benign hills of Hobbiton are found near Matamata; Mounts Ruapehu and Ngauruhoe play Mount Doom; Ringwraiths ride through Wellington's town belt; the Arrow river becomes the Ford of Bruinen; Lake Wakatipu hosts Lothlorien; the Ida Valley becomes the Plains of Rohan; and the Southern Alps are omnipresent.

New Zealanders also dominate the cast and crew. On screen,

there are familiar faces everywhere you look. Bruce Hopkins, Robbie Magasiva, Craig Parker, John Bach, Noel Appleby, Marton Csokas, Peter Tait, Harry Sinclair, Alistair Browning and Joel Tobeck appear. And there could have been more: Sam Neill and Russell Crowe were considered for lead roles; Lucy Lawless was cast as Galadriel but had to withdraw when she became pregnant.

Thousands of New Zealanders were extras. Broadcaster Paul Holmes was an Orc. Bret McKenzie, later to rise to fame in *Flight Of The Conchords*, became an internet icon after a brief, silent appearance as an Elf in *The Fellowship Of The Ring*. Members of the New Zealand army were engaged as extras for the Battle of

The Lord Of The Rings
2001–2003 / Feature
557 mins
DIRECTOR / **Peter Jackson**
PRODUCERS / **Peter Jackson, Barrie Osborne, Fran Walsh, Tim Sanders**
SCREENPLAY / **Fran Walsh, Philippa Boyens, Stephen Sinclair, Peter Jackson**
PRODUCTION COMPANY / **New Line Cinema/ WingNut Films**

the Black Gate. Ten thousand cricket fans at the Wellington stadium provided the Orcs' bloodthirsty cries for the Battle of Helm's Deep.

The figures are mind-spinning. At times up to seven crews were at work on the film simultaneously; total workers numbered nearly three thousand. The Battle of Helm's Deep took four months to film – all at night. The dead Oliphant carcass was the largest prop ever built for a movie. Over 19,000 costumes were made by the wardrobe department, and 1600 pairs of prosthetic Hobbit feet by Weta Workshop. Most notably, there were 2827 digital effects.

To render the character Gollum, Weta Digital developed a new technique, 'subsurface scattering', creating realistic translucent materials in wholly digital form. Such meticulous attention to detail was emblematic of the production. Some actors learned and spoke Elvish. Props were finely wrought, even if – as with the etchings on Sauron's armour – they would be viewed for only a few seconds. And great attempts were made to be true to Tolkien's descriptions: every domestic item, costume and weapon was designed specially for the production, with Alan Lee, the famed Tolkien illustrator, on board as concept artist. *The Lord Of The Rings* was, quite simply, mighty storytelling and fantasy on a scale never attempted before in the history of world cinema.

The Lounge Bar

TOO MANY NEW ZEALAND SHORT FILMS fail in the last seconds – the resolution is muddied or the punchline not delivered correctly. Wonderful quarters of hours are diminished by a few seconds. Not so *The Lounge Bar*, which is complete and circular and a little like a cinematic matryoshka doll. This is what the Front Lawn (Harry Sinclair and Don McGlashan) always did best – comedies of manners with linear narrative entwined like spaghetti.

Anyone who can wail the lyrics of their album *Songs from the Front Lawn* will know the plot of *The Lounge Bar* from its theme tune: 'There's a man at the bar staring into space … The man at the bar has lost his memory, the man at the bar could be anybody.' 'I could be anybody,' says the man at the bar: the film's running joke has the dialogue match the song playing on the jukebox.

Wearing an extraordinary and absurd head brace, the man clearly has a drinking problem – he keeps spilling them, cocktail umbrella and all. How he came to be found in the harbour with a fractured skull, how the hired musician became the barman, and how the lemon knife came to be broken are explained with deft and witty shifts of time.

The narrative cuts to the past. Hadley, the manager, has hired a musician ('Hey,' he says, 'do you know the one that goes "There's a man at the bar staring into space?"') who arrives with bell-bottoms and sideburns. Hadley later makes an inept pass at

The Lounge Bar
1988 / Short / 12 mins

DIRECTOR / **Harry Sinclair**
PRODUCER / **Grant Campbell**
SCREENPLAY / **Don McGlashan, Harry Sinclair**
PRODUCTION COMPANY / **Front Lawn/Sycorax**

the barmaid ('Ngaire, you're really spunky'), and this leads to a violent confrontation.

Like the Front Lawn's *Walkshort*, *The Lounge Bar* is an utterly satisfying, inventive film. Peter Jackson helped contribute the special effects.

Lovelock

JUST AS LEON GAST'S 1996 documentary *When We Were Kings* focussed on a few seconds of an historic boxing bout between Muhammed Ali and George Foreman, David Robertson's *Lovelock* illuminates the vital moments of the 1500-metre final at the 1936 Berlin Olympics. Jack Lovelock (born in Crushington; educated at Timaru Boys' High and Oxford University) ran a perfect race, surging once, surging again, then using his legendary kick to win gold in front of Adolf Hitler beneath flapping swastikas.

Lovelock's strict training regimen, strategising and the race itself are filmed in chiaroscuro by Donald Duncan, recalling Leni Riefenstahl's fascist film *Olympia*, which documented the same games. Crispin Balfour, with his stark black singlet with its oversized silver fern, his upright running action and his tight curls, could have stepped straight from a grainy Pathé newsreel, but it is the race that is the star: rarely has a fiction film portrayed a sports event with such authenticity. The glances and stares between Lovelock and his surly American opponent Glenn Cunningham are a dramatic silent conversation.

Stuart Hoar's pared script hints at possible reasons behind Lovelock's mysterious death years later under a New York subway train, but Robertson's great achievement is to create resonances and advance the narrative with brief but telling images and details. The moments before Lovelock's death – the light of the oncoming

Lovelock
1992 / Short / 15 mins

DIRECTOR / SCREENPLAY / David Robertson
PRODUCER / Bruce Sheridan
PRODUCTION COMPANY / Stratford Productions

train, the tannoys, the rubbish blown along the tunnel, the watch with his race time engraved – are echoed in the flash bulbs of photographers and the gaping tunnels of the Olympic Stadium as the story shifts decades and continents. The film ends with a coup de cinéma, a brilliant exclamation mark to a superb visual and historic statement.

Magik And Rose

THE SUCCESS OF AUSTRALIAN FILMS *Strictly Ballroom* and *The Castle* in the '90s led to a swathe of quirky comedies being commissioned this side of the Tasman. But where *Jubilee, I'll Make You Happy*, *Via Satellite* and *Savage Honeymoon* didn't quite succeed, *Magik And Rose*, the story of an unlikely friendship between two women who are both anxious to be pregnant, does.

Part of the film's appeal is its strong sense of place. Its setting in Hokitika, among whitebaiters, square dancers and a wildfoods festival, is fertile ground for comedy. Indeed this West Coast setting, location of the grim drama *Bad Blood*, challenges Sam Neill's theory of New Zealand film-making as the cinema of unease: the Southern Alps don't loom but smile majestically, and Hokitika's streets are presented as friendly, not threatening.

However, the principal reason for the movie's success is its strongly written characters, who have just enough grit, nuttiness and humanity for us to believe they could really be found on Hokitika's electoral roll. Nicola Murphy (*Jack Brown Genius, The Hole*) is totally convincing as the small-town pharmacist's assistant. Simon Ferry (*Out Of The Blue, Home Movie*), as her husband, adds sensitivity and depth to a potentially two-dimensional portrayal of a typical Kiwi bloke.

The supporting cast is good, particularly Oliver Driver (*Snakeskin, Black Sheep*), as a fractal geek and snail-breeder – a one-man

Magik And Rose
1999 / Feature / 92 mins

DIRECTOR / SCREENPLAY / Vanessa Alexander
PRODUCER / Larry Parr
PRODUCTION COMPANY / Kahukura Productions

essay on the sexiness of thin men in underpants. Florence Hartigan is convincingly cast as Magik's estranged daughter, as voluble and smart as her biological mother.

There are superb one-liners throughout the script, which juggles the pathos and comedy inherent in the process of human reproduction. And as well as wonderfully comic set pieces, such as Rose walking home in Magik's bizarre outfit and interviews with sperm donors, when dealing with the complex relationships between mother and daughter, and husband and wife, this film has a real solidity.

Magik And Rose is not perfect. The resolution happens too quickly, some acting is stolid, and credibility can be strained. This can all be forgiven for Vanessa Alexander's achievement in corralling a marquee-full of wildfoods revellers to complete the last reel over just two days.

The Maori Merchant Of Venice

FOR DECADES NEW ZEALAND SCHOOLCHILDREN endured long, earnest BBC productions of Shakespearean plays. These had stilted action, no visual fireworks, and looked for all the world like filmed versions of stage plays. In the last twenty years things have looked up. Since 1990 there have been three film versions of *Hamlet* on general release, and many of Shakespeare's plots have been cleverly contemporarised. *Romeo And Juliet* has been set in south-central Los Angeles. *Richard III* has been rebranded a fascist dictator. Shakespeare himself has been made a romantic hero in *Shakespeare In Love*.

Like all these, *The Maori Merchant Of Venice* is a huge advance on the BBC efforts, and while it doesn't match the popularity and accessibility of Kenneth Branagh or Baz Luhrmann's adaptations, it is a monumental work on many levels – not least because it is the first full-length, big-screen sound version of the play to be attempted. Equally remarkable, it is the first Maori-language feature film.

It was largely due to the efforts of Don Selwyn that the film was made. Selwyn's legacy to New Zealand cinema is threefold – as a character actor (*Sleeping Dogs, Lost Tribe, Mauri*), as a fosterer of Maori talent for film and television, and as a producer. *Feathers Of Peace* and *Don't Go Past With Your Nose In The Air* were two of his successes, but *The Maori Merchant Of Venice* is his magnum opus.

Selwyn had promised the noted historian and translator Pei Te

Hurinui Jones that he would stage Jones' 1945 Maori translation of the play, and this finally happened during the New Zealand sesquicentennial in 1990, fourteen years after Jones' death. From there it took another ten years to convince funding bodies that a film version was worthy of support.

The film has vestiges of the stage performance. The final court scene was filmed at the Church of the Holy Sepulchre on Auckland's Khyber Pass Road, where the play was first performed, the unscripted interjection of a kuia in the audience was retained, and Waihoroi Shortland reprises his stage role as Hairoka (Shylock). Shortland dominates the second half of the film. So intense is his performance that he overshadows otherwise competent turns by other male leads. Ngarimu Daniels shines as Pohia (Portia). Among the extras is veteran Ramai Hayward.

What is most impressive is the mixing of Venetian and Maori

The Maori Merchant Of Venice
2002 Feature 158 mins

DIRECTOR **Don Selwyn**
PRODUCER **Ruth Kaupua**
WRITER
William Shakespeare
TRANSLATOR
Pei Te Hurinui Jones
PRODUCTION COMPANY
He Taonga Films

symbols. The Italianate buildings of Auckland suggest the bustling canal city but Pohia wears curved pounamu, the Prince of Morocco is greeted with a karanga and wero, traditional Maori wind instruments are heard amid the beautiful soundtrack, and Hairoka demands utu.

The subtext of the play unavoidably concerns colonialism, racism and justice. The only pakeha actors play English and Scottish lords, Anatonio's boat and the church both hail from the colonial era, and the final demand by Hairoka for the contract to be carried out has a sense of grievance familiar to Maori seeking the honouring of the Treaty of Waitangi. The fateful deal between Hairoka and Anatonio is concluded in front of a painting by Selwyn Muru that has the word 'holocaust' burning from the canvas.

This is a long film, and at times uneven. Some passages feel declaratory, and the direction and camerawork do not always come to the actors' assistance. Overall, though, it is a triumph of language, chiming out theatre's greatest words in rich new timbres.

Meet The Feebles

MEET THE FEEBLES IS NOT the nastiest movie ever made in New Zealand – *Death Warmed Up* would probably scoop that award. Nevertheless, it is the kind that should be announced with a warning siren, or come packaged with disinfectant. It includes a fornicating walrus, a fly who gets tortured, and a disastrous finale

Meet The Feebles
1989 / Feature / 96 mins

DIRECTOR / **Peter Jackson**
PRODUCERS / **Peter Jackson, James Booth**
SCREENPLAY / **Peter Jackson, Fran Walsh, Stephen Sinclair, Danny Mulheron**
PRODUCTION COMPANY / **WingNut Films**

involving a song called 'Sodomy'. This is *42nd Street* meets *Death Wish* – with strings attached.

Bletch the walrus is the manager of a puppet troupe riddled with problems: the knife-throwing frog is a junkie with Vietnam trauma; Sidney the elephant is trying to evade a paternity suit from Sandy the hen; and Lucille the poodle is caught in flagrante delicto with Trevor the Rat, who makes porno flicks – one is called *Came A Hot Friesian*. The glamour of theatre attracts Wobert the Hedgehog, but he is too naïve to appreciate that the Feebles are more vile than vaudeville.

Meet The Feebles is wildly inventive and technically brilliant. Puppets play golf and drive stretch minis. One-liners are spread around like chlamydia, and there are ironic references to *Casablanca*, *The Godfather*, and (when Wynyard the frog is caught by Vietcong rabbits) the Russian roulette sequence in *The Deer Hunter*.

This is a great, gross film, and often so sick it should be watched in quarantine. As one reviewer noted, it was unfortunate Peter Jackson had already used the title *Bad Taste*.

Memory And Desire

THE PLOT OF *MEMORY AND DESIRE*, the courageous debut feature of writer/director Niki Caro, follows Sayo, a Tokyo office lady. Sayo is accustomed to the fact that she is plain: she describes herself in a voice-over as a 'Christmas cake' – inedible after the 25th. However, when she meets a handsome and younger salaryman, Keiji, an unlikely and 'unsuitable' romance begins. In Sayo, Keiji sees a joie de vivre that is absent from his structured life.

Memory And Desire is based on a short story by Peter Wells, itself inspired by a true story reported in the media. Sayo and Keiji elope to New Zealand, where they marry. Their honeymoon is a bus trip through a damp landscape of mock-Tudor motels. Australian cinematographer Dion Beebe, who gave Rotorua an oppressive lushness in Alison Maclean's 1992 thriller *Crush*, here charges New Zealand's tourist trail with erotic danger.

As the newlyweds struggle to consummate their marriage, their bubble of optimism is pricked. Finally, in a cave on a lonely beach, Keiji carves the kanji for 'love' on a rock, and the couple have sex. Soon afterwards, he drowns.

There are problems with *Memory And Desire*. It comes as a shock when Japanese characters speak English to each other in Tokyo, and absurd when there is a translator involved, and the pace slows so much that the film sometimes feels like a slide show.

When Sayo (Yuri Kinugawa) returns to Japan a widow and, as

tradition dictates, lives with her mother-in-law, the narrative picks up speed again. There is a strong contrast between Keiji's mother's mannered mourning and Sayo's overwhelming sense of loss, and the mother can barely contain her dislike of her daughter-in-law. Tokyo now seems cramped and artificial, its only 'wilderness' a kitsch love hotel. Sayo flees back to New Zealand and the cave, where she can live with Keiji's memory.

Memory And Desire
1998 / Feature / 89 mins

DIRECTOR / SCREENPLAY / **Niki Caro**
PRODUCER / **Owen Hughes**
PRODUCTION COMPANY / **Frame Up Films**

Memory And Desire has arresting images, and an elegance and detachment you could mistake as quintessentially Japanese if you didn't know it was directed by a New Zealander. Kinugawa admirably portrays Sayo's tenacious spirit and unravelling sanity, and the film was selected for Critics' Week at Cannes.

Middle Age Spread

AMID THE FONDUE SETS, coffee-table books and floral patterns of an urban, middle-class home of the 1970s lie strong emotions – love, frustration, disappointment, cynicism, lust and lack of fulfillment. Colin has been elevated to school principal, but seeks to break from the confines of middle age with a fitness regime and infidelity with a relief teacher. His home life with the intelligent but bored Elizabeth has long since become jaundiced. A dinner party, from hors d'oeuvres to nightcaps, becomes the forum for not just reverie but revelation.

Middle Age Spread was the first New Zealand feature since the Second World War to be billed a comedy, and the first to be set entirely in an urban environment. Its wit and verbal fireworks make for an entertaining ride, but the satirical cannon is firmly trained at the bourgeois audience, who are meant to squirmingly identify with the pretensions and posturing of the characters, and the mid-life crises on display.

Keith Aberdein's screenplay breaks easily from its origins in Roger Hall's stage play: while the dinner party stays at the heart of the film, we also see Colin at school functions, at the pub with his cynical friend Reg, and at the small flat of his lover, Judy. We wait deliciously for the emotional landmines to explode.

Colin is Grant Tilly's finest turn. From his hilarious jogging that opens the film to his famous last line 'What we do now is the dishes', he is masterful. His delivery of pithy one-liners is so understated he never seems like a character, more like a colleague or neighbour. His portrayal of his affection for Judy is totally convincing, his resigned state at the movie's coda a triumph of pathos.

Middle Age Spread
1979 / Feature / 94 mins

DIRECTOR / John Reid
PRODUCER / John Barnett
SCREENPLAY / Keith Aberdein
PRODUCTION COMPANY / Endeavour Productions

You can gauge the success of this film by comparing it with Mike Leigh's television adaptation of *Abigail's Party* (1977), which also deals with middle-class mores in the context of a soirée. *Abigail's Party* is often considered the zenith of British television, yet *Middle Age Spread* is as emotionally intense, hums with more humour, and leaves its stage origins much more successfully.

Mr Wrong

THE MOST REMARKABLE FEATURE of New Zealand cinema is its large number of women directors. Vanessa Alexander, Gillian Ashurst, Jane Campion, Niki Caro, Christine Jeffs, Alison Maclean, Nicky Marshall, Merata Mita, Christine Parker, Athina Tsoulis and Sima Urale have all directed feature films in recent decades, while Rachel Anderson, Jessica Hobbs, Rebecca Hobbs, Zia Mandviwalla, Fiona Samuel, Annalise Patterson, Jane Shearer, Reina Webster and Katie Wolfe have directed short films that have attracted awards or plaudits.

The list has its genesis in two feature films made by women directors in the mid 1980s. Yvonne Mackay's *The Silent One* has status as the first New Zealand fiction feature directed by a woman; *Trial Run* by Melanie Read and Gaylene Preston's *Mr Wrong*, released soon afterwards, marked the arrival of women as auteurs.

Trial Run and *Mr Wrong* both tackle the thriller genre from a strong feminist perspective. For *Trial Run*, Read tried to employ as many women as possible – seventy-five percent of the crew were female. Thriller conventions are subverted: the female 'victim' fights back; home is not a place of safety; there is no knight in shining armour; women are shown in traditionally male roles. However, the film suffers from a poor finish: the supernatural element is poorly integrated, and the resolution confusing and unsatisfying.

Mr Wrong is a more complete thriller. Meg (Heather Bolton) buys a Jaguar Mark 2, only to discover it is haunted by the spirit of a murdered woman. She tries and fails to sell the car, and is stalked by a sinister figure.

Bolton is believable and engaging, and while not as actively independent as *Trial Run*'s Rosemary, also defies the Hollywood convention that a heroine must be glamorous. Seemingly naïve when conned into buying the car, she rapidly becomes self-aware, and prepared to use her wits to solve the frightening situation in which she finds herself. There are no Mr Rights to help her: the men are inept (Wayne), drunk and threatening (Bruce), patronising (Clive), or gay (Mr Whitehorn). She learns self-defence, and

Mr Wrong
1985 / Feature / 89 mins

DIRECTOR / Gaylene Preston
PRODUCERS / Robin Laing, Gaylene Preston
SCREENPLAY / Gaylene Preston, Graeme Tetley, Geoff Murphy
PRODUCTION COMPANY / Preston Laing Productions

memorably carries a miniature Venus de Milo as a weapon when confronting an intruder.

Mr Wrong successfully mixes the terrifying with the banal. There are some excellent, suspenseful scenes, such as when the face of the ghost is slowly revealed from newspapers Meg is using as wrapping paper, and a haunting incident at the top of Paekakariki Hill. The climax also spooks perfectly with the surprise appearance of Mr Wrong himself.

The Navigator: A Medieval Odyssey

VINCENT WARD, described by critic Philip French as 'an antipodean Werner Herzog', is one of New Zealand's great visionaries of cinema. Whether it's a couple making love on top of a blimp (*Map Of The Human Heart*), computer-generated wonders of the afterworld (*What Dreams May Come*) or vibrant battle scenes (*River Queen*), his images can be breathtaking in their beauty and emotional power.

Ward's characters often have vivid imaginations as well. Toss in *Vigil* has a strong sense of fantasy. Chris in *What Dreams May Come* not only goes to paradise when he dies, but believes he can rescue his wife Annie from hell. Griffin, *The Navigator's* young English peasant from the thirteenth century, has nightmarish hallucinations as the Black Death claims villages around his home.

Griffin's visions include a journey through the Earth to a celestial city where, to fend off the pandemic, he will forge and erect a copper cross for the city's cathedral. That the city is Auckland in the twentieth century and the pilgrims must tunnel through the planet imbues *The Navigator* with magic, terror and dramatic irony. Once they get to the other side, the six medieval Cumbrian villagers must survive a motorway and a nuclear submarine before negotiating the spire of the minster. (Ward conceived the idea for the film while trapped on the median strip of an autobahn.)

This extraordinary film is an allegory, a musing on faith and fra-

The Navigator: A Medieval Odyssey
1988 / Feature / 93 mins

DIRECTOR / **Vincent Ward**
PRODUCERS / **Gary Hannam, John Maynard**
SCREENPLAY / **Vincent Ward, Kely Lyons, Geoff Chapple**
PRODUCTION COMPANY / **Arenafilm/Film Investment Corporation**

ternity, with black and white cinematography reminiscent of Ingmar Bergman's dream sequence in *Smultronstället* (*Wild Strawberries*). The modern images, including a shop window full of television sets and a pilgrim's ride on a locomotive, are like a Boschian vision of hell.

But all is not doom and gloom. There are delightful

scenes as the thirteenth-century Cumbrians meet twentieth-century blacksmiths who are facing their own apocalypse – their foundry is due to be closed. Shared humanity makes seven millennia evaporate.

This is a well-cast movie. Hamish McFarlane (*An Angel At My Table, Larger Than Life*) is impressive as Griffin, and Marshall Napier, Paul Livingston, Bruce Lyons and Noel Appleby do a good job as the adventurous pilgrims. (Appleby, a bit actor, was appropriately discovered working for the Auckland City Council's drainage department.)

Part of the miracle of *The Navigator* is that it got made at all. As with many Vincent Ward movies, the shoot was difficult; some scenes were filmed in a part of the Southern Alps accessible only by helicopter. The project was dogged with financial problems – and, ironically, a virus ravaged cast and crew.

The Newest City On The Globe

A LOVE POEM to Peter Wells' hometown of Napier, *The Newest City On The Globe* is a beautiful film. Ostensibly a documentary about creating a model city after Napier's buildings were extensively damaged in the 1931 earthquake, it is in reality a captivating fantasy.

In real life, the reconstruction of the city in the Spanish style of Santa Barbara 'where hotels are haciendas' stalled for lack of finance, but that has not stopped Wells vividly imagining how things might have been. As narrators Donogh Rees and Michael Hurst breathily intone that 'this is not Napier as it is but seems to be', a swing band plays in silhouette in the city's sound shell. Fountains are incandescently lit. A Bogart figure leans against a colonnade and smokes.

The art deco wonders of the city centre become part of a movie set – 'a forgotten Hollywood backlot'. An illuminated Criterion Hotel is imagined with bellhops, women in satin dresses, and a harlequin in masque. The Masonic Hotel and Daily Telegraph building play their part in lush tableaux. The camera lingers on deco features – door handles, windows, light fittings – as martini glasses jingle portentously.

Behind the camera, Leon Narbey finds beauty everywhere: his time-lapse shots as the day's changing light paints the treasures and clouds scud across the sky are memorable.

The city's history before the earthquake is portrayed through rhythmic and inventive editing of colonial-era images – the women in crinolines and men in busbies appear to move – while the film's poetic script reports that Napier was founded with 'characteristic economy', creating brittleness that would be so apocalyptically exposed in the great shake.

The Newest City On The Globe
1985 Documentary
27 mins

DIRECTOR WRITER
Peter Wells
PRODUCERS Peter Wells, Stewart Main

This is a companion piece to *The Mighty Civic*, Wells' 1989 paean to the Queen Street movie palace, in which, as here, history, actuality and fiction are stylishly blended.

Ngati

NGATI HOLDS A RECORD as the world's first feature film written and directed by members of a minority indigenous race. The cast and crew, recruited from a film course, were almost exclusively Maori. The production's immersion in the East Cape community where it was filmed added to the experience of collective effort.

The film was an active attempt by writer Tama Poata and director Barry Barclay to portray – in style, content and production – what it is to be Maori. Their goal was largely met. This is a study, without melodrama or sentimentality, of an entire community, and rarely has a film evinced the rhythms of life so believably.

Ngati's narrative is almost passive. A boy is dying of 'a Maori sickness', a local abattoir where many of the community work may close, and a handsome young Australian-born doctor arrives and begins to find out about his heritage. There is no dramatic event to propel the story forward, and few characters follow the conventional Hollywood arc. But a sense of permanence and timelessness makes *Ngati* feel like a snapshot: events happened before the curtain rises, and will continue in similar vein after the credits roll.

The arrival of the doctor (Ross Girven) sets up a potential conflict. His racial prejudice fades soon after arrival when the community embraces him at the pub, but there is a clash of cultures around which treatment is best for the sick boy – western medicine or the skill of the tohunga?

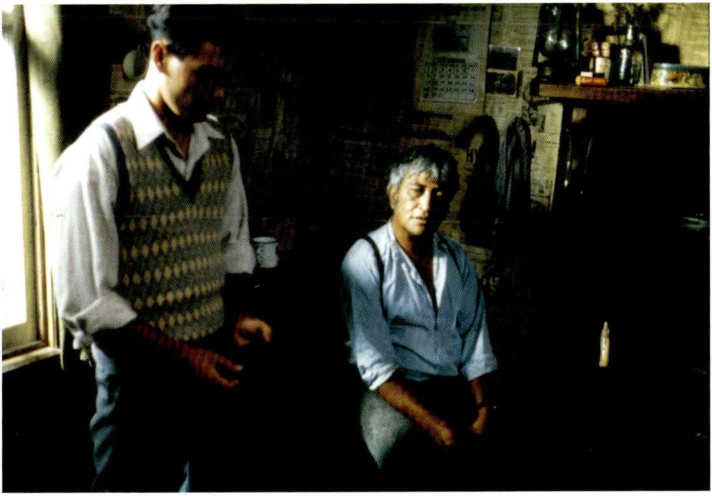

Ngati
1987 / Feature / 93 mins

DIRECTOR / Barry Barclay
PRODUCER / John O'Shea
SCREENPLAY / Tama Poata
PRODUCTION COMPANY / Pacific Films

The key moment in the movie is the speech by Sally (Connie Pewhairangi) to the officials of the meat company, a proclamation of antonomy and self-sufficiency. Her assertion that local Maori could run the factory is backed up by the solidarity displayed as the community gathers and industriously prepares food for the meeting.

In spite of lightness of plot and some amateurish acting, *Ngati* is gripping drama. Judy McIntosh and Wi Kuki Kaa shine and Barclay shows his willingness to defy movie convention by having the film's burgeoning love story consummated with a peck on the cheek. He defied other conventions too: *Ngati* was not initially released on general distribution but shown first in marae across the country.

Once Were Warriors

ALAN DUFF'S NOVEL on which this film is based begins with a tirade of insults. The cinema version, contemporised and moved to Auckland, starts off no less jarringly. The camera pulls back from a billboard celebrating the scenic beauty of New Zealand to reveal an urban jungle of tarseal and concrete, and the lead character, Beth Heke, negotiating this grim environment.

Most New Zealanders saw *Once Were Warriors*: it became the highest grossing local film of all time and surpassed *Jurassic Park*. For many of the audience, seeing it was a confrontational experience: they were forced to face either a New Zealand with which they had had little contact, or harsh truths about what was occurring within their own community. Patch-wearing gang members wept in the aisles. Hui were organised to examine the subject matter.

This subject matter includes the effects of colonisation and Maori urbanisation, the oppression of women and, overwhelmingly, domestic violence. The violence almost subsumes the text. Lead character Jake's early bashing of a bystander in a pub sets it at the forefront, adding fragility and tension to every scene in which Jake appears, an effect enhanced by low camera angles when his wrath rises. Jake's explosion when his wife Beth refuses to cook eggs still shocks, no matter how many times you have seen the movie.

In spite of a budget of only two million dollars, this is an exceptionally well-made film. Rena Owen, as Beth, puts in arguably the

greatest female performance in a New Zealand film to date. In a tour de force matched in emotional complexity only by Bruno Lawrence in *Smash Palace* and *The Quiet Earth*, she manages to convince us that it is possible for her to feel affection for Jake despite his brutal treatment of her – until her final defiant speech.

Once Were Warriors
1994 / Feature / 102 mins

DIRECTOR / **Lee Tamahori**
PRODUCER / **Robin Scholes**
SCREENPLAY / **Riwia Brown**
PRODUCTION COMPANY / **Communicado Productions**

With the sheer physicality of his performance as Jake, Temuera Morrison managed to wipe the association most of the audience had with him as genial doctor Hone Ropata in television's *Shortland Street* and redefine his career. The supporting cast is equally good, particularly Mamaengaroa Kerr-Bell as Gracie and Cliff Curtis as Bully. Riwia Brown's script is a huge achievement, converting Duff's stream of consciousness into a film, and the soundtrack impresses with its guitar squalls and ominous bullroarer.

There are some flaws: Bully's beating seems to celebrate vigilantism, gang members are glamourised, and characters' grim surroundings are photographed in rich hues. But director Lee Tamahori deliberately made the movie look polished so as not to alienate audiences, and it's true it would not have been as affecting or popular had it not been for its excellent production values.

The success of *Once Were Warriors* meant Tamahori was lost to New Zealand film-making. Attracted to Hollywood and its excesses, he would have commercial success with James Bond, *xXx* and *The Sopranos* franchises, but would not again scale the critical heights of his New Zealand masterpiece.

Out Of The Blue

IT SEEMED AN IMPOSSIBLE PROJECT – a feature about New Zealand's worst modern-day killing spree. The massacre at the small sleepy seaside town of Aramoana in 1990, the moment when dwellers in lean-tos and cribs were dragged into the world of AK-47s, seemed too raw, too recent. But director Robert Sarkies and Bill O'Brien, author of the book on which the film is based (and Dunedin police communications officer at the time of the tragedy), show great sensitivity in this earthy, unromantic portrayal of the residents and the devastation that beset them.

Neighbours argue about the loudness of music. A dog goes missing. Washing is hung out. Yet the film is at times elegiac. On this spring evening, boys cycle, adults fish, kites are tugged in the breeze. The violence to be visited on these people seems unimaginable.

Out Of The Blue succeeds in focussing on a plethora of characters. Some of the story is told from the perspective of a young policeman, Nick Harvey (Karl Urban), but the film works best when focussing on the people of the town – Jimmy and Helen Dickson, the Bryson and Holden ménages – and killer David Gray's sparse shack and chaotic mind.

Gray's journey to Dunedin builds a picture of mental instability. When children on the bus laugh, he presumes they are laughing at him. At a bank, he reacts angrily because of a misunderstanding. In a gun shop he is polite and respectful. His psyche is swinging wildly. Matt Sunderland (*Nature's Way, Woodenhead*) gives a terrific performance as the loner slipping towards murderous rage with each slight.

The violence, when it finally begins, is observed from a distance, and with a strange ordinariness. There are no vicarious thrills in David Gray's stalking through the town, just the bravery and compassion of the victims. In some of the most affecting scenes, elderly Helen Dickson crawls to speak to a wounded man, and Nick Harvey cradles a three-year-old girl shot in the stomach.

Out Of The Blue
2006 Feature 103 mins

DIRECTOR Robert Sarkies
PRODUCERS Tim White, Steven O'Meagher
SCREENPLAY Graeme Tetley, Robert Sarkies
PRODUCTION COMPANY Southern Light Films/ Desert Road Films

Patu!

PATU!'S TAG LINE – 'You might like it, you may hate it, you might even be in it' – says it all. Made at a time of national trauma, the film documents one of the most divisive periods in New Zealand's recent history – the protests surrounding the 1981 tour of the country by apartheid South Africa's national rugby team, the Springboks.

Merata Mita and her crew of camerapeople – principally Barry Harbet, but also Gaylene Preston, Waka Attewell, Roger Donaldson, Leon Narbey, Alun Bollinger and Alister Barry – braved often violent scenes to capture this transfixing historical record. Using

the innovative style she employed in *Bastion Point Day 507* (1980), Mita lets the action tell the story; there is little exposition or context given. Many views – most notably shots from among the phalanx of protesters occupying Rugby Park in Hamilton and surrounded by baying rugby fans – had not been seen on mainstream news media. Negatives of some of the material had to be sent out of the country to prevent confiscation by the authorities.

The documentary eschews talking heads – Donald Woods, a South African journalist, is one of only two brief interviews to camera. Instead, Mita thrusts the viewer into earnest meetings of protest organisers Andrew Beyer, Trevor Jones and John Minto, and hui with Maori activists Donna Awatere and Syd Jackson.

This is a highly political work, and there is authorial intent in every scene. From the beginning, images of South Africa's infamous Sharpeville massacre are interspersed with footage of anti-tour protesters on Auckland's Queen Street. People who support the tour are cast as racists by their own invective – 'Nigger lover'

Patu!
1983 Documentary
113 mins

DIRECTOR / PRODUCER
Merata Mita
PRODUCTION COMPANY
Awatea Films

and 'How would you like your daughter to marry one of them?'

The collected images are startling: a bold lingering shot between the narrow front-line of armoured police and crash-helmeted protesters at Christchurch; the tuxedo-clad property developer Bob Jones making an obscene gesture; barbed wire fences and shipping containers barricading Eden Park. Twice, the cinematographers themselves are attacked, and sounds of truncheons and winces of pain are clearly heard.

The film's greatest achievement, apart from the fact it was actually made, is its skilful editing. Images resonate or clash with each other to create an impressionistic history, whether it is clowns armed with baguettes, street theatre by school kids, protesters facing down police, or the Mongrel Mob marching ominously into the fray.

There is a subtle subtext in the recurrent use of the national anthem, 'God Defend New Zealand': the versions change until the final portentous electronic rendition is slowed until barely recognisable. There is also ironic use of Sibelius's *Karelia Suite* as a Cessna flies low over Eden Park, dropping flour bombs: the music was the theme of *This Is New Zealand*, a popular film commissioned by the government to lure tourists to New Zealand.

Patu! may be agitprop but it is remarkable agitprop – a voice, angry, intelligent and Maori, from beyond the establishment.

The Piano

NOT A CENT OF NEW ZEALAND MONEY went towards making *The Piano*, but this is indubitably a Kiwi film. A New Zealand story told by a New Zealander, writer-director Jane Campion, it examines a crucial time in the history of immigration – the moment of landfall, when Europeans set foot on an alien shore and attempted to forge a new life here. A ferocious West Coast swell opens the movie, dank nikau forest hinders the characters as they travel inland, and New Zealand Hollywood stars Sam Neill (*Sleeping Dogs, Omen III*), Anna Paquin (*Amistad, X-Men*) and Cliff Curtis (*Star Wars, Three Kings)* appear.

The quality of the performances and the handsomeness of Stuart Dryburgh's photography set *The Piano* apart. The three principal adult characters are bold and vulnerable at different times. Stewart (Neill) jealously guards his land and his wife, but reveals himself as terribly lonely. Baines (Harvey Keitel), a sensualist, baulks at debasing the woman he loves.

Ada (Holly Hunter), the object of their attentions, is a mute, impassive and stoic Scot who speaks only briefly – in voice-over. Yet in spite of being transferred between men like a chattel, she emerges as strong and independent, a gothic heroine akin to Jane Eyre, Rosamond Vivian or Hester Prynne. Her story is told largely through what we see, which is often little more than the tight weave of her bun, or the entanglement of vines that is a metaphor

The Piano
1993 / Feature / 122 mins

DIRECTOR / SCREENPLAY / Jane Campion
PRODUCER / Jan Chapman
PRODUCTION COMPANY / CIBY 2000/Jan Chapman Productions

for her entrapment in an unhappy marriage.

The Piano tends towards erotic melodrama, but never capsizes into a camp bodice-ripper, largely because of the psychological complexity of the story and Campion's cinematic vision.

There have been millions of academic words expended on the film. Critics have examined inconsistencies in the narrative; the complex sexuality, which includes voyeurism, rape, sadism and masochism; the cartoonish representation of Maori; and the ambiguous ending. Most viewers, however, have been happy to be swept away by Michael Nyman's remarkable score, by breathtaking images such as Anna Paquin as Flora dancing with kelp, a whalebone-corset tent on the beach, and Ada collapsing like a dirigible into mud, and by the lushness of piano lesson scenes, where a hole in a stocking is intensely erotic.

The Piano is so far the only New Zealand film to have won a Palme d'Or at Cannes. (In 2009, Jane Campion would nearly repeat the feat with *Bright Star*, her moving portrayal of the poet John Keats' doomed love affair.)

The Piano went on to take an Academy Award for best original screenplay. (Comedian Raybon Kan quipped that the script probably consisted of, 'There is mud. Ada says nothing.') Eleven-year-old Anna Paquin deservedly won an Oscar for best supporting actor, famously reaching the podium out of breath and stunned, which is how many of the audience felt as the film's credits rolled.

Punitive Damage

IN 1991, a twenty-one-year-old New Zealander, Kamal Bamadhaj, was killed during a massacre by Indonesian troops in Dili, the capital of East Timor. It was the second university holiday he had spent working as a human rights activist in the occupied nation.

Bamadhaj was a handsome and intelligent young man – his charisma and passion are evident in the way his mother, sister and girlfriend talk about him in this film – but the work is not as much about him as about the quest of his mother, Helen Todd, for justice – in particular her pursuit through the American justice system of the Indonesian military commander who had ordered the attack on the gathering of independence protesters.

Documentary-maker Annie Goldson frames the story around reconstructions of the actual court transcripts. A potentially clumsy device, this proves surprisingly effective. It is supplemented by snapshots and news footage that elucidate East Timor's horrific recent history; images of the massacre itself, filmed by cameraman Max Stahl, are particularly powerful.

However, it is the interviews with Timorese eyewitnesses, with American journalist Alan Nairn, one of the last westerners to see Kamal alive, and with Todd in her Malaysian home that really resonate.

The skill with which Goldson manages to draw out the media-shy Todd is remarkable. Todd's quiet recitation is extremely moving

because of its lack of visible bitterness or anger: openly subsuming her loss within that of the families of the 270 Timorese also killed in the massacre, she is focussed, articulate and compassionate. She relates matter-of-factly the political obstructions she met in trying to retrieve her son's body, and there is implicit criticism of the Suharto regime, the New Zealand government and the resistance movement Fretilin.

This is a sensitive work, neither manipulative nor exploitative. Goldson, who is also a university academic, is known for making documentaries with strong social and political undercurrents. She has documented the feminist movement of the 1970s (*Sheilas*), the plight of the Afghani *Tampa* refugees (*Pacific Solution*), and most recently the murder of gay Red Cross worker John Scott in Fiji (*An Island Calling*).

Punitive Damage
1999 / Documentary / 77 mins

DIRECTOR / WRITER / **Annie Goldson**
PRODUCERS / **Annie Goldson, Gaylene Preston**
PRODUCTION COMPANY / **First Run/Icarus Films**

All are compelling works, but *Punitive Damage* is a stand-out. Released on the cusp of East Timorese independence, it serves as a monument to Bamadhaj, Todd, and the many thousands of others who fought to end Indonesia's rule over the former Portuguese colony.

The Quiet Earth

BRUNO LAWRENCE WAS THE FACE of New Zealand cinema for the best part of a decade. Between 1980 and 1986 he was in the cast of fifteen feature films, half of all those made. Whether it was his riverbed voice, his brown eyes or his mastery of expression, Lawrence made pattern baldness sexy.

The Quiet Earth is his finest moment. At the encouragement of the director, Geoff Murphy (*Goodbye Pork Pie, Wild Man*), the producers hired Lawrence instead of an American star such as Jack Nicholson, as they had intended. As Zac, Lawrence carries the movie alone for the first half-hour. He is the last man on Earth: a failed project has extinguished all other life. There are no animals, no movement, simply the silence of an uninhabited planet. The loneliness, euphoria and madness that follow the cataclysm are brilliantly portrayed by Lawrence – most spectacularly wearing a silk slip and wielding a shotgun as he wanders into a church in search of God.

Of all New Zealand's archetypal men alone, Zac is the most alone – until Joanne (Alison Routledge) arrives. When another survivor, Api (Peter Smith), also makes an appearance, a triangle of race and gender develops. Unfortunately, however, the sexual rivalry weakens the dramatic flow. As film critic Helen Martin wrote: 'Joanne overdoes the "Playing God" idea to the point that, last woman on Earth or not, she might be outstaying her welcome.'

The trio realise that they were all at the point of death when the apocalyptic 'Effect' occurred. Zac, as a scientist involved with the project that caused it, feels he has been 'condemned to live'. His search for redemption gives Lawrence the chance to display his acting ability as a man of action, and drives the narrative towards its exciting and explosive climax.

The Quiet Earth is based on a 1981 novel by Craig Harrison, and in the political context of the time it was seen as a cinematic comment on the breakdown of relations between the stridently anti-nuclear New Zealand government of David Lange and the intransigent Reagan administration. While the film could be filed

under 'political allegory' or 'science fiction', it is equally a character study, an exposition of existentialism, and a rollicking action movie in which a hero must beat a countdown.

The depopulated world is beautifully realised and the sets are superb: an incredible 92 locations were used. Care was taken by Murphy to wipe the soundtrack, removing all background noise and creating a disconcerting absence. John Charles' score, played by the New Zealand Symphony Orchestra, is notable.

The movie is bookended by two remarkable scenes – an eerie sunrise, which opens it, and a beach scene, which not only closes it but provides one of the most jaw-dropping moments in New Zealand cinema to date.

The Quiet Earth
1985 Feature 91 mins

DIRECTOR Geoff Murphy
PRODUCERS Sam Pillsbury, Don Reynolds
SCREENPLAY Sam Pillsbury, Bruno Lawrence, Bill Baer
PRODUCTION COMPANY Cinepro/Pillsbury Films

Rain

THIS DEBUT FEATURE about a family spending a summer holiday at their bach and slowly unravelling due to drinking, infidelity and the speed wobbles of the daughter's advancing sexuality has an almost hypnotic quality – enhanced by the use of slow-motion shots that lurch into a drunken wooziness as the parties roll on.

The story is anchored in the 1970s with vivid period touches – tall beer bottles, vintage porn magazines, patterned dresses and push mowers. Christine Jeffs and cinematographer John Toon give everything the washed-out look of a tattered photo album. In this ostensible paradise, everything, including the landscape, has an aura of threat and decay. The summer is not going to end happily.

Developed from a short but detailed novella by Kirsty Gunn, *Rain*'s plot is secondary to impressions and atmosphere. The narrative is driven by glances, glares, stares, and the occasional terse phrase. And although the film is clad in retro neutrals – the bach interiors are suffused with tan and brown – it is also oddly sensual: there is seduction and jealousy over the cocktail cherries.

Alicia Fulford-Wierzbicki (*Fracture*) is remarkable as coquettish thirteen-year-old Janey. Trapped between childhood and the adult world, she plays merrily with her young brother, Jim, until she observes her mother's infidelity with reptilian photographer Cady (Marton Csokas). Still defiantly a girl, her body years from

Rain
2001 / Feature / 92 mins

DIRECTOR / SCREENPLAY / **Christine Jeffs**
PRODUCER / **Philippa Campbell**
PRODUCTION COMPANY / **Communicado/Rose Road**

full maturity, Janey seeks to usurp her mother in Cady's affections, and this leads to some of the film's, and indeed New Zealand cinema's, most shocking moments – Janey's casual lighting of a morning cigarette, the Lolita-like way she wields a martini glass, and her embrace with and violation by Cady. And this is not the only great performance: Aaron Murphy is spirited and natural as Jim, while Sarah Peirse and Alistair Browning are brilliant as the curdling couple.

Rain is a lament for innocence. The slow-motion shot as the excoriated family drives away from Mahurangi Bay to the soundtrack of Neil Finn's ululation is the essence of melancholy.

Rain Of The Children

NEW ZEALAND FILM-MAKERS have not made many films about films. Geoff Steven examined the entrepreneurism, exploitation and incompetence of pioneer director Alexander Markey in 1985's *Adventures In Maoriland*, but Costa Botes' behind-the-scenes look at *The Fellowship Of The Ring* seems likely to remain on the shelves, tangled in legal issues.

This makes *Rain Of The Children* a rarity. The sense that it is a unique objet d'art is enhanced by the extent to which director Vincent Ward inserts himself into the action.

"STUNNING"
"Masterful...a haunting historical epic...compelling...mythic in its sweep"
HOLLYWOOD REPORTER
"Emotionally rewarding...imaginative...stylish...powerful...and heart wrenching"
VARIETY
"Incredibly moving"
SYDNEY FILM FESTIVAL
FROM THE DIRECTOR OF VIGIL, THE NAVIGATOR AND MAP OF THE HUMAN HEART
A VINCENT WARD FILM
RAIN OF THE CHILDREN

Rain Of The Children
2008 / Feature / 102 mins

DIRECTOR / SCREENPLAY / Vincent Ward
PRODUCERS / Vincent Ward, Marg Slater, Tainui Stephens
PRODUCTION COMPANY / Forward Films

The film tells the story of Ward's return to the place where he filmed a forty-minute documentary, *In Spring One Plants Alone*, in 1980, when he was a long-haired nascent cineaste. Now half a century old, Ward examines his affection for Puhi, the stooped octogenarian subject of that film, and builds a narrative around the notion that she was under a makutu, or curse.

This is a nearly unclassifiable film – mystery, ghost story, historical reconstruction and visual poem, with lashings of biography, autobiography and tribal history. Awkward interviews with Puhi's whanau are mixed with some extraordinary set pieces. The vision of Tuhoe people under torchlight climbing Maungapohatu is astounding, as is the detailed depiction of Maori prophet Rua Kenana's New Jerusalem, his city in the mist where Puhi grew up. Seven actresses, including *Once Were Warrior*'s Rena Owen, play Puhi, while Temuera Morrison, Taungaroa Emile and Waihoroi Shortland have cameos.

This is not just a redux of Puhi's life, unearthing the grief that burdened her, but a renaissance of Ward after the notorious off-screen dramas of his 2005 feature *River Queen*. Whether it is the horror of the 'body tree', the police raid on Rua's community, or the shot of a naked unconscious Niki watched over by his white horse, it is clear that the years have not diminished Ward's unusual ability to compose images.

The Road Back

ANNALISE PATTERSON EXPLORED her Maori identity in *Black Bitch* (1994). Here she turns her attention to her Yugoslav heritage, specifically her grandmother who, to adapt to a new life in the Antipodes, was encouraged to submerge her Balkan identity.

The film was inspired by writer Amelia Batistich meeting 'the saddest woman in the world', a Dalmatian who had lived on Northland's kauri-gum fields in isolation from other women. In *The Road Back* it is 1910. Croatian immigrant Vinka spends her life alone in a hut in a far north forest. Her husband comes home exhausted after digging for gum. There is tenderness between them, but also bitterness. Vinka demands: 'Find me a woman for talking.' She thinks they have found 'the wrong America'. She carries a mirror everywhere; sadly her reflection is the only female face she sees.

On a walk to a beach she imagines she sees in the mirror a group of women from her own country singing a folk song. The vision embodies the female camaraderie she craves, and the culture and customs she misses. Then, among tall toi toi plants, she discovers a tent and inside it an Indian woman (Manesha Patel). These two lonely women have no common language, but in a magical sequence that void is crossed: the Indian woman adds joy and colour to Vinka's life. Vinka promises to return the next day, but when she does the woman has disappeared. Perhaps she has moved on – or perhaps she was never there. Either way, the road back to companionship and cultural identity has been lost.

Vinka is played with a mantle of sorrow by untrained actor Ana Jankovits, who herself escaped the war in the Balkans to emigrate to New Zealand. The cinematography occasionally takes the breath away, and fragments of Eastern European language and music, phantoms from a faraway home, haunt the soundtrack.

The Road Back
1996 / Short / 15 mins

DIRECTOR / SCREENPLAY
Annalise Patterson
PRODUCER / **Rachel Jean**
PRODUCTION COMPANY
Frame Up Films

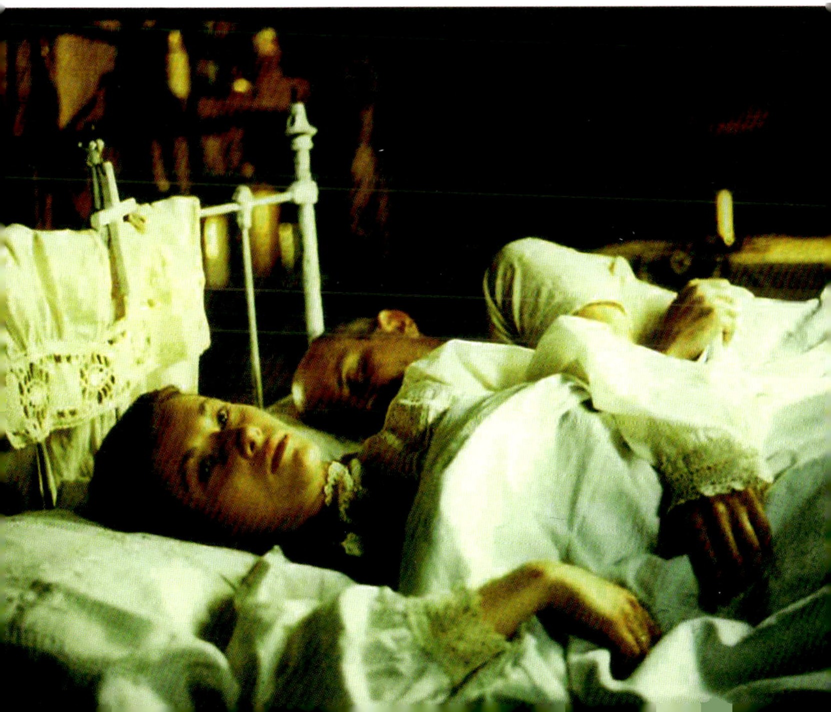

Ruby And Rata

RUBY AND RATA is a 110-minute riposte to anyone who claims New Zealand cinema is dour and grim. Ruby, an octogenarian landlady, wants to rent the bottom floor of her Mount Albert home to an Anglican career woman. Instead she gets Rata, fraudster, solo mum, and lead singer of a band called Apocalypse.

The great achievement of *Ruby And Rata* is that it largely avoids caricature and sentimentality. As tenants, Ruby and her son Willie, a misbehaving urchin, are totally believable, with Willie becoming the glue that holds the two women together. Willie, Ruby's 'little spaceman', may think their landlady is a witch but the pair develop an unlikely friendship as people marginalised by everyone else. Ruby tells Willie stories, feeds him chocolate fish, and produces magic from a crystal glass. Willie gets a sense of belonging that he hasn't previously enjoyed.

This leads to a domestic war between the two women, but in spite of Ruby's prejudice and Rata's dissembling and fakery, you end up rooting for both sides. This is because *Ruby And Rata* is, at its heart, a satire on the 'new right' economic philosophies of the 1980s and the social fragmentation they caused. Whether up against bureaucracy, ageism or obnoxious relatives, Ruby, Rata and Willie have to fight for security in a world of greed and 'user pays'.

The hilarious dialogue is often delivered so matter-of-factly it is easy to miss treasures such as, 'She knows more lies about me than anyone else!' There are exquisite scenes – Willie sitting on Ruby's lap driving a car, dancing with her, arriving through her bathroom window with a flashing helmet – and some memorable acting. Yvonne Lawley is winning as Ruby, mentally sprightly even as age makes her physically vulnerable. Lee Mete-Kingi is marvellous as Willie: his fake smile in the social welfare office is a comic highlight. And Simon Barnett as Ruby's exploitative and inept nephew shows excellent timing with physical comedy and malapropisms.

Ruby And Rata
1990 / Feature / 110 mins

DIRECTOR / **Gaylene Preston**
PRODUCERS / **Robin Laing, Gaylene Preston**
SCREENPLAY / **Graeme Tetley**
PRODUCTION COMPANY / **Preston Laing Productions**

Runaway

RUNAWAY IS AN ODD FILM. From the jazz overture to the speedboating across the Hauraki Gulf and the gig (Ray Columbus and the Invaders) attended by the jaded main character, New Zealand is depicted as a world away from the familiar six o'clock swill and free school milk of the real 1960s.

David Manning, a handsome hedonist who scowls for the first twenty minutes, commits a minor fraud in order to retain his faux lifestyle. As it turns out, this leads to an epiphany. To avoid criminal charges, Manning drives to the Hokianga and finds a more 'authentic' life, including fishing and carpentry. However, things quickly unravel when he falls for Laura, a vampish Eurotrash housewife, and loses the chance of a relationship with a local girl, Isobel, played by a coy young Kiri Te Kanawa.

After a mud-fight with Laura in the mangroves, more charges are laid and David is forced to flee, heading south in a stolen car. After several unfortunate encounters with law enforcement, and a driver who has a cardiac arrest, the runaway takes the inter-island ferry, where he meets Diana. There seems to be a chance of happiness, but time and again he and Diana are forced to flee.

Runaway lacks narrative cohesion, a clear moral message and even authenticity – some dialogue was dubbed so New Zealand accents could be neutralised. However, it did drag New Zealand cinema into the modern era. There are numerous evocations of

Runaway
1964 Feature 102 mins

DIRECTOR PRODUCER
John O'Shea
SCREENPLAY **John O'Shea, John Graham**
PRODUCTION COMPANY
Pacific Films

contemporary European film, and influences of the New Wave and Italian director Michelangelo Antonioni are obvious. O'Shea took a print of Antonioni's *L'Avventura* on location and the crew watched it repeatedly as inspiration for coming scenes.

Colin Broadley as David looks like a knitwear model, but the existential angst that drives the narrative is sensitively delivered. His relationship with Diana (beautiful Deidre McCarron) is convincing even if their dialogue is not. Kiri Te Kanawa's brief role would have been more expansive but for some prudishness towards a bedroom scene and an ill-timed bout of facial eczema. Author Barry Crump makes a sinister appearance as a lecherous hunter.

Tony Williams' cinematography in this film is at times magical. From the opening shot of Diana's face to the looming glacial rocks at the end, there is texture and atmosphere a-plenty. Robin Maconic's unobtrusive score swells to majestic organ figures as David walks to insignificance across the Southern Alps.

Runaway is disjointed. Ideas were not carried through because of difficulties during filming, and there are narrative holes. Even so, it has a style and sophistication not seen previously.

The Sadness Of The Post-Intellectual Art Critic

WEIGHED DOWN WITH A PRETENTIOUS TITLE, this film has become universally known as *Art Man*. Scripted from dreams in the manner of Luis Buñuel, it is, as is evident from the start, anchored in a very unusual world. As the opening credits reveal contributions from Martyn Sanderson, Alister Barry, Alun Bollinger, Euan Frizzell and Vincent Ward, Jonathan Besser's discordant soundtrack plays. A red flare billows smoke past Daliesque eyes. Eugene Ionesco is quoted. It all makes for strange, dislocating viewing.

An art critic (the director, George Rose) begins to deliver a lecture direct to camera in the mode of Simon Schama or Kenneth Cumberland. As he rants against the intellectualisation of art he is overwhelmed by images of his first sexual encounter and other aspects of his early life.

There is much to like in this film. Sure, the action is patchy and regularly flops from the sublime to the ridiculous. The acting of Rose (and Richard Adams as his clownish alter ego) is sometimes overwrought. But the dream sequences are often staggeringly gorgeous, the textures of shifting sand on the beach and the camera panning through the dream house past table legs, gramophones and doll parts are a bravura mélange of cinematography and sound design, and the art critic's final monologue as he has a grand mal mental breakdown is superbly scripted and acted.

Art Man was fuelled by anger at the conservative art scene, and aptly came face to face with reactionary values at the Auckland International Film Festival: a screening at the Civic Theatre was cancelled ten minutes before it was to begin as the cinema owner considered the full-frontal nudity pornographic. There was a near riot in the full house. The film was finally screened at a nearby blue movie theatre.

The Sadness Of The Post-Intellectual Art Critic
1979 / Feature / 45 mins

DIRECTORS / **George Rose, Richard Adams, Martyn Sanderson**
PRODUCER / **George Rose**
SCREENPLAY / **George Rose, Richard Adams**

The Scarecrow

HAWERA'S RONALD HUGH MORRIESON was a bon vivant, womaniser and heavy drinker. Born in 1922, during his lifetime he left south Taranaki no more than half a dozen times. Instead he was content to observe the passions and perversities of provincial New Zealand. He began writing at the age of forty, and peeled off four novels before his health began to collapse. In 1972, the year he died, he stated that he didn't want to be 'one of those buggers who gets discovered after they're dead'. It was a self-fulfilling prophecy – within fifteen years three of his novels would have been made into films. The best of these is *The Scarecrow*.

The novel begins with one of the best lines in New Zealand literature: 'The same night our fowls were stolen, Daphne Moran had her throat cut.' The film channels the spirit of that line, juxtaposing the ordinary and the horrific. The fictional town of Klynham, which bears more than a passing resemblance to Hawera, is fecund with lust and depravity just beneath the veneer of respectability. Uncle Athol steals his nephew's chooks, there is sly-grogging and card games, and Prudence Poindexter's sexuality becomes the focus of attention of every male unrelated to her, from Les with his blatant desire, to senile, bedridden Mr Fitzherbert, who attempts rape with the complicity of his wife.

The arrival of real malevolence in the form of necrophiliac killer Hubert Salter – who announces himself by whispering chillingly,

'I am Death' – moves this towards a true gothic fable. The film is, however, just as concerned with the Poindexter household, and particularly young Ned Poindexter's confrontations with the Lynch gang, as it is with the activities of a serial killer. This is, after all, Ned's memoir, and the local bullies are a much more immediate source of fear.

Veteran American import John Carradine (*Bride Of Frankenstein, Stagecoach*) is a wonderfully cadaverous Salter. He had to be – he received $20,000 of the film's limited budget. With his lined face and gnarled fingers he appears to be just another of the town's eccentrics and grotesques, yet his monologue as he holds a knife against Prue's 'lush virginal body' is hair-stiffeningly creepy.

Sam Pillsbury evokes the time and place with great period detail. *Broken Barrier* is playing at the cinema, jaffas roll under the seats,

The Scarecrow
1982 / Feature / 88 mins

DIRECTOR / Sam Pillsbury
PRODUCER / Robert Whitehouse
SCREENPLAY / Michael Heath, Sam Pillsbury
PRODUCTION COMPANY / Oasis Films/New Zealand National Film Unit

the Salvation Army band appeals for temperance outside the pub, and a half-moon is cut in the door of the outdoor dunny.

Overall, though, *The Scarecrow* is less a thriller than a burlesque tale of boys' rites of passage – Dickens with flattened vowels. By the end the boys have been initiated into the prurience and vices of the township. Salter's presence has been smoothed over, like his final burying place. Klynham remains much the same.

Second-Hand Wedding

NEW ZEALAND HAS BEEN CALLED a nation of first-time directors. Since the 1970s the pattern has been repeated: a director makes one or two feature films that function as business cards and then moves overseas – usually, although not always, to Hollywood. This has been (more or less) the story of Roger Donaldson, Vincent Ward, Jane Campion, Scott Reynolds, Niki Caro, Lee Tamahori, Christine Jeffs and Geoff Murphy.

Hollywood has also hoovered up young talent such as Andrew Adamson (*Shrek*, *The Lion, The Witch And The Wardrobe*) and Andrew Niccol (*Gattaca*, *The Truman Show*). With each migration, technical knowledge and ability are lost to the local film industry.

Second-Hand Wedding, directed by Paul Murphy, challenges that paradigm. Murphy is the son of Geoff Murphy, who spent years directing big-budget movies in Hollywood before returning home to work as second-unit director on *The Lord Of The Rings* trilogy. This suggests not only that a film-making dynasty may be developing in New Zealand, but that the migration of talent is not always permanent.

Paul Murphy, who graduated to film-making from directing television ads and shows, grew up amid the creative anarchy of Bruno Lawrence's Blerta community, and picked up some of his knowledge of entertainment by osmosis. The yellow Mini that ploughs down Kapiti Coast streets in his film's opening scenes can be seen as not just homage to his father's *Goodbye Pork Pie*, but a four-wheeled family crest.

Second-Hand Wedding
2008 / Feature / 98 mins

DIRECTOR / **Paul Murphy**
PRODUCERS / **Nigel Stanford, Paul Murphy**
SCREENPLAY / **Nick Ward, Linda Niccol**
PRODUCTION COMPANY / **Garage Sale Productions**

Luckily, though, *Second-Hand Wedding* does not ape the demented comedy of *Goodbye Pork Pie*. To the contrary: its success is in its restraint. It may celebrate such kiwiana as paua, garden gnomes and John Rowles, but it also embraces another New Zealand trait – laconic, understated humour. The 'happy couple' and their workmates are endearingly normal, and Geraldine Brophy and Patrick Wilson convincingly underplay their roles as garage-sale magpies and parents of the bride.

The movie is not without faults. There is an ill-conceived dream sequence, a couple of characters seem like plot culs-de-sac, and the viewer occasionally feels sedated rather than seduced. But overall the warmth is infectious, and the dramatis personae so familiar you feel you shouldn't complain in case you offend the neighbours.

The infection spread across the nation: more people saw *Second-Hand Wedding* than the six other local feature films released that year put together. It sped up the chart of top-grossing New Zealand films of all time, breaking the one-million-dollar mark in its first five weeks – and even overtaking a certain 1981 movie about a yellow Mini.

The Singing Trophy

A CABIN-FEVERISH HUNTER has a fine trophy wall of stuffed and mounted animals – a ferret, a couple of pheasants, a buffalo, and a boar he shot 'eating his last breakfast'. He fills the long evenings drinking flagons of home brew, eating pickled onions, and conducting Johann Strauss's 'Blue Danube' in his head, using as a massed choir the menagerie he has killed. The high C, however, eludes him – until he spies a mouse, and the game is afoot, literally and figuratively.

Grant Lahood of *Snail's Pace* and *Chicken* again works with animals. Oscar has an athletic role as the fleeing mouse, expertly filmed while eluding his pursuer. Peter Tait (*Carry Me Back, Kitchen Sink*) is excellent as the good keen man whose predatory plans are continually thwarted, and who has evidently spent too many long winter nights on his own. Most of the six lines of dialogue are addressed to his dog.

The Singing Trophy
1993 / Short / 13 mins

DIRECTOR / SCREENPLAY
Grant Lahood
PRODUCER **John Keir**
PRODUCTION COMPANY
Keir and Cox Productions

This black critter comedy was the first New Zealand short to be nominated for a Palme d'Or at Cannes. Taut, suspenseful and funny, it comes with a gross climax, and an easily missed coda.

Sione's Wedding

FIRST THERE WERE FILMS about Pacific Islanders in a palagi environment (*Sons For The Return Home, Other Halves*) and stories of Samoa made by New Zealanders (*Flying Fox In A Freedom Tree, The Silent One*). Then came *Sione's Wedding,* and the beginning of true New Zealand Pasifika cinema. The four characters are both P.I. and Aucklanders, and the tension between the values of these two communities provides much of the conflict and a lot of the comedy.

The film opens with Feelstyle's song 'I Do Believe'. Aerial shots pan across Auckland, the biggest Polynesian city in the world. Four young Samoan men, Michael, Albert, Stanley and Sefa, known to themselves as the Duckrockers after their 1990s' break-dancing troupe, suffer from a Peter Pan complex. They're in their thirties, but are still behaving like unruly teenagers. Then a McGuffin is added: all four have been banned from the wedding of Michael's younger brother, Sione, because of serial misadventures, shown on video by the pastor of their church. The ban will be waived only if they can find partners to take to the wedding.

This is easier said than done. Albert has never had a girlfriend, Michael is a hormone in cycle shorts, Sefa has a partner but arrives home at dawn one too many times, and Stanley is fixated on chat-lines and opportunities for short-term romance.

This is old-fashioned comedy: shot mostly in Grey Lynn, it

could equally have come from Ealing or Hollywood. Everybody will end up happy, but there will be a few hoops to jump through on the way.

Wit, camaraderie and well-timed repartee sizzle. Throw in some spirited physical comedy from the talented Oscar Kightley, dancing from Iaheto Ah Hi that is worth the price of admission alone, and the antics of Derek (D-Rizzle), the try-hard gangsta, the overofficious security guard, and Leilani's siblings, and you have an enjoyable romp. But it is the awkwardness of Albert around his beautiful cousin and the believability of the relationship between Sefa and Leilani that gives this film some (but not too much) depth.

Sione's Wedding
2006 / Feature / 97 mins

DIRECTOR / **Chris Graham**
PRODUCERS / **John Barnett, Chloe Smith**
SCREENPLAY / **James Griffin, Oscar Kightley**
PRODUCTION COMPANY / **South Pacific Pictures**

Skin Deep

WHEN GEOFF STEVEN FOLLOWED the 1975 land hikoi as a cameraman for the documentary *Te Matakite O Aotearoa*, he passed through Raetihi in the Waimarino. The town's colonial facades and wide streets, designed so a bullock team could do a U-turn, seemed like a Hollywood backlot. Fascinated, Steven returned and made an experimental three-screen video presentation, *Aspects Of A Small Town.*

Fast forward, and Steven and co-writers Pier Davies and Roger Horrocks decide to use this prime location for a satire about provincial boosterism, conformity and hypocrisy. However, they have no desire to exploit small-town mores for easy laughs. They develop sympathetic three-dimensional characters. Their film, *Skin Deep*, evolves into subtle comedic drama, passing insightful social comment without being didactic.

The town's burghers plan to attract industry and tourists though a vacuous television campaign and the importing of a big-city masseuse. Bob, a businessman and head of the Progressive Association, wants to expand the masseuse's job description to include 'extras'. Ken Blackburn is brilliantly unctuous as this wheeler-dealer cloaked in civic respectability but unmasked behind the closed doors of the massage parlour. Grant Tilly is his equal as Phil, a disillusioned man struggling with his infatuation for the masseuse, Sandra. When he replays Sandra's dictaphone rendition of 'I Want To Be Loved

Skin Deep
1978 / Feature / 103 mins

DIRECTOR / Geoff Steven
PRODUCER / John Maynard
SCREENPLAY / Geoff Steven, Piers Davies, Roger Horrocks
PRODUCTION COMPANY / Phase Three Films

By You' he is simultaneously creepy, pathetic and touching. Deryn Cooper as Sandra, the masseuse who hopes she has left behind the seedy side of her profession, exudes a weathered magnetism.

To give the film the feel of a documentary, Steven and the cameraman, Leon Narbey, used available light, actual locations, unglamorous actors and often untrained extras. Free beer was offered to entice locals into the pub scenes, boxer Monty Betham Snr and entertainers Bunny Walters and Beaver appear as themselves, and Bob Harvey plays a metropolitan advertising executive, which is exactly what he was. The boom operator who allows the microphone to dip into shot occasionally is none other than Lee Tamahori, who would go on to fame and fortune as a Hollywood director.

Camera movements are slow and long takes preferred – there is only one close-up in the entire movie. The camera keeps its distance, and often holds a shot after the action finishes, leaving us looking at the usually unpopulated and static setting.

This subtle, soberly paced film is an essay on civics and civility, but some of its absurd moments – a jogging club bouncing up and down in the council chambers, a woman in a bunny-girl costume painting a fund-raising thermometer – could be happening in real life near you. The authentic feel of *Skin Deep* and its discreet satire initially disconcerted some viewers: they didn't realise they were watching a comedy.

Sleeping Dogs

SLEEPING DOGS WAS THE FIRST 35-millimetre colour fiction feature made in New Zealand and is the Rosetta Stone of New Zealand cinema. Before it, a feature film on such a scale did not seem possible. After it, the industry developed all the way to Peter Jackson standing on the podium at the Academy Awards.

Based on C.K. Stead's 1971 novel *Smith's Dream*, the film depicts a dystopian future in which a fascist government runs New Zealand

as an American puppet state. Smith (Sam Neill), a Kiwi as ordinary as his name, abandons Auckland for a contemplative life on an island off the Coromandel Peninsula after he discovers his wife has been unfaithful with his best friend. Once there, he becomes an accidental terrorist, reluctantly involved in conflict between a group of rebels and the government's Special Police.

In spite of its political livery, this is an action film and follows the conventions. The title conveys threat, the poster, with words bleeding into an AK-47, foregrounds the violence, and there are the usual escapes, shoot-outs and car chases.

However, whether it was because of the participation of the Royal New Zealand Air Force with its fighter jets and helicopters, or the images of crash-helmeted police, *Sleeping Dogs* captured the imagination of the film-going public and banished cultural cringe. More than 250,000 New Zealanders saw it on its initial release, and it became the first New Zealand feature to get an American cinema release.

Local audiences warmed to the familiarity. Well-known broadcaster Dougal Stevenson reads the news, the Hauraki Gulf shines luminously, moreporks cry, and characters flee down Auckland streets. Indeed, while filming a scene where Smith escapes from a prison van, Sam Neill was tackled by a passerby.

As Smith, Neill has the handsome blandness of an everyman. He prefers not to talk about politics and religion. Even while wielding firearms against government commandos he is ambivalent about the conflict. Ian Mune, as the man who cuckolded him, is a vibrant and energetic presence, even if he does take an entire reel to die.

The movie's message is somewhat muddled. Director Roger Donaldson, an Australian who had come to New Zealand to dodge the draft for the Vietnam War (and would later go on to success in Hollywood with films such as *No Way Out* and *Dante's Peak)*, departed from the source novel by having Smith involved with the guerillas to the very end. The film seems to be saying that no one can separate themselves from the conflict, but resistance is bound to fail. Smith's final defiant one-fingered salute may be iconic, but it is a futile gesture.

Sleeping Dogs
1977 / Feature / 107 mins

DIRECTOR / PRODUCER
Roger Donaldson
SCREENPLAY / Ian Mune, Arthur Baysting
PRODUCTION COMPANY
Aardvark Films

A Small Life

A REMARKABLE COLLABORATION between director Michael Heath, composer David Downes, director of photography Stephen Latty and performers Mahinarangi Tocker and Kelly Lede-Tropman, *A Small Life* is a deeply emotional song cycle that portrays the last days of a terminally ill boy's life. In so doing, it delves into deeper, more primal emotions than are usually explored in the musical genre.

The film begins with the mother (Tocker) keening on the shores of Lake Ferry in the Wairarapa. Everything the film will succeed in delivering is obvious in this first scene. The composition of the shot is striking, the music hauntingly beautiful, and the mother's grief tangible. The story is told principally through the images and song lyrics. Incidental dialogue is rarely audible, and only the occasional voice-over interrupts the music. The outside world seems a long way beyond the hills and trees surrounding the cottage where mother and son live. Tama, the boy, listens to strange Chinese and Indian voices on the wireless. There are just two visitors – a social worker and a postman.

Downes' music and soundscapes are impressive. Action songs display the joyous filial bond. The frail voice of Lede-Tropman intones in recitative style. Tocker whirls a purerehua, a bullroarer, to soothe the sick child. Her strong singing as she mourns takes on an other-worldly quality.

The digital video-camera work of Latty matches the sound design in its aesthetic achievement. As Tama rushes across farmland with his oversized Swanndri flapping, he is viewed from behind a dirty window. When he collapses, the poplars rock like ululating women. When his body is swaddled in a shroud, the camera itself seems wrapped in a veil.

A Small Life
2000 / Feature / 50 mins

DIRECTOR / SCREENPLAY / **Michael Heath**
PRODUCERS / **Stephen Latty, Michael Heath, David Downes**
PRODUCTION COMPANY / **Gumption Films**

Tama's last moments, when he hallucinates that he is at a children's party and imagines his father arriving, are both uplifting and terribly sad. Only the most stoic will not grieve. This small yet remarkable film is probably New Zealand's finest musical.

Smash Palace

ROGER DONALDSON'S *SLEEPING DOGS* may have kicked off the new wave of New Zealand film, but his second feature, *Smash Palace*, was its first masterpiece. From the opening sequence, in which a car leaves the Desert Road and topples dramatically to Sharon O'Neill's soundtrack, to the sucker punch ending on the rail tracks, this is a vivid, passionate and tragic tale of a marriage falling apart and the impact on a seven-year-old child.

The film is a masterpiece not only because it wrestles courageously with difficult subject matter, but because it contains two of the most astonishing acting performances in New Zealand cinema history. If there were any justice, Bruno Lawrence would have been festooned with awards for his work as the taciturn former racing driver and archetypal male Al Shaw. Despite his character's appalling behavior, which includes armed robbery, kidnapping and sexual violation, Lawrence manages to retain the audience's sympathy. His brown eyes seem homely and vulnerable. His love for his little girl, Georgie, shines through. His confusion at the situation in which he finds himself is obvious from the moment that, side-lit, he leans against a shotgun. He comes across not as a psychopath, but as a man driven to irrational behaviour by a complex cocktail of love and jealousy, and the threat of losing his beloved daughter.

The other remarkable performance is by Greer Robson as

Georgie. At just nine years old, she is never less than convincing.

Cinematographer Graeme Cowley used the naturalism of East European cinema and the distinctive, empty landscape photographs of Robin Morrison as touchstones for lighting this film. The tiny alpine township of Horopito enhances the isolation of Shaw's French wife Jacqui, the great sky broods, and the enormous car graveyard provides for stunning compositions – and some rather unsubtle symbolism. This marriage is a wreck, rusting fast.

There are some tremendous scenes. Al posts his clothes through Jacqui's letter box. Locals yodel. Georgie flicks a torch on and off in response to the violence in her home. A makeshift birthday party in the caravan is full of tenderness and heart-breaking pathos.

Smash Palace was first released in overseas cinemas, in the

Smash Palace
1981 / Feature / 108 mins

DIRECTOR / PRODUCER /
Roger Donaldson
SCREENPLAY / **Roger Donaldson, Peter Hansard, Bruno Lawrence**
PRODUCTION COMPANY /
Aardvark Films

expectation that foreign success would encourage New Zealanders to go and see the film when it was released at home. The strategy worked: *The New York Times* chose *Smash Palace* as one of the ten best films of 1981 and local audiences poured in.

Snakeskin

AMONG NEW ZEALAND FILMS, only *Forgotten Silver* has celebrated the pure joy of cinema as much as *Snakeskin*. References to *Thelma And Louise*, *Wild At Heart* and *Star Wars* show that, while *Snakeskin*'s main characters live in Christchurch, they have been soaking in stateside pop culture. They desire Route 66, stetsons and a Ford T-Bird. What they get is the back road from Yaldhurst to Methven, a '73 Chrysler Valiant with its top cut off, and lots of dialogue that would sound corny if it were not intended to be.

Director Gillian Ashurst's love for cinema is both a bane and a boon. The plot writhes like a serpent in the second half, trying to swallow too many genres and finally eating its own tale. Nevertheless, this is an effortlessly cool road movie that indulges in the imposition of American road-movie iconography on New Zealand's prosaic reality, and contains passages of fine writing.

Two twenty-something fantasists, Alice (Melanie Lynskey) and Johnny (Dean O'Gorman), pick up Seth, an American hitchhiker who is wearing snakeskin boots and has enemies on his tail. He also has drugs and a gun. Alice and Johnny enjoy the frisson of the role-play – until things start going bad. Alice contemptuously calls New Zealand 'the safest fucking country in the whole world', but as the trio drive towards our own wild west, the chocolate-box Canterbury landscape starts to look rather sinister, and the village of Otira a frontier town where showdowns occur.

As dusk falls and the body count rises, the movie veers off course: a supernatural element seems attached by Blu-Tack, and a subplot in which comedy duo Taika Waititi and Jodie Rimmer drive a Mr Whippy van sits uneasily with the macabre tone.

However, *Snakeskin* has its consummate moments, including an encounter with wandering stock, the rendering of an acid trip by a spinning camera, a drive through a sea of sunflowers, grubby sex on the floor of a toilet cubicle, scary movements of road signs and tattoos, and an incident in which a skinhead, Speed, (played by Oliver Driver in a splendidly unhinged performance) breaks into a house and contorts in a woman's slip. Boyd Kestner (*Hannibal*, *Knots Landing*) is malevolent and muscular as the hitchhiker cowboy, while Lynskey is sexy and watchable – many miles from her outsider plainness as Pauline Parker in Peter Jackson's 1994 movie *Heavenly Creatures.*

The film's revelation is not only that New Zealand is not as benign as Alice thought, but also that its iconography is powerful: a yellow Mini picks up Alice while she is hitchhiking; she watches a New Zealand western, *Para Recordar*; and 'Bigger Than Texas', the alt-country song that opens the movie, is not from Nashville's finest but Dunedin's Renderers.

Snakeskin
2001 Feature 92 mins

DIRECTOR SCREENPLAY
Gillian Ashurst
PRODUCER **Vanessa Sheldrick**
PRODUCTION COMPANY
Cowgirl Productions

Someone Else's Country

IT IS AXIOMATIC that New Zealanders do not talk about politics and religion: to be public about political beliefs in particular seems vaguely distasteful. New Zealand film-makers do not share this ambivalence. Whether it be *Fighting Back, The Bridge, Wildcat, Bastion Point Day 507, The Neglected Miracle, The Kaipara Affair, Patu!* or *The Last Resort*, they spear-tackle political subjects, usually with a left-wing or Maori focus.

Alister Barry's trilogy *Someone Else's Country, In A Land Of Plenty* and *A Civilised Society* is a powerful set of films examining the effect of 'new right' economic policies on New Zealand. The first film is a broad history, the second hones in on employment and the third on education. These documentaries become increasingly sophisticated in their construction, but it is the first angry roar – *Someone Else's Country* – that has become an underground classic.

Starting with images of the 1973 coup d'état in Chile, Ian Johnstone, in his English brogue, connects the privatisation (at the barrel of a gun) of state-owned assets under General Augusto Pinochet with the free-market philosophies and sale of public assets by the democratically elected Labour government of 1984 to 1990. This is a clumsy juxtaposition, but Barry is not going to compromise his message just to be stylish.

In 1996, thousands flocked to see the film at the New Zealand

International Film Festival. State-owned Television New Zealand refused to broadcast it because of its lack of balance, but videocassettes circulated throughout the country. By the time TVNZ finally relented eight years later, an estimated 75,000 people had already seen *Someone Else's Country*. Researching for this book at the New Zealand Film Archive, it was the film I saw more people watching than any other.

Its popularity stems from a collective desire to make sense of the rapid and often devastating economic changes that took place in the 1980s and '90s, first under Labour minister of finance Roger Douglas, and then under the National government of 1990 to 1996, when Ruth Richardson clasped the purse strings.

Someone Else's Country
1996 / Documentary / 109 mins

DIRECTOR / WRITER /
Alister Barry

PRODUCER / PRODUCTION COMPANY /
Community Media Trust/ Vanguard Films

Barry has described this film as 'old-fashioned … no whizzy graphics'. That is true enough. Extensive use is made of news footage, including David Lange's 1987 'cup of tea' speech – the moment when Roger Douglas's reforming wings were clipped – and a hilarious incident where Richardson and National prime minister Jim Bolger complain about the murkiness of water in a carafe as Richardson's tough 'Mother of All Budgets' is announced. Spliced throughout are interviews from a Greek chorus, including unionist Helen Kelly, Alliance leader Jim Anderton, and even Michael Laws who, in an oddly gripping turn, rains scorn on his former National Party colleagues.

Neat editing makes fun of Richard Prebble and Jim Bolger as they contradict themselves, but there is little fun to be had as monetarist ideology is pursued to stark ends and ordinary citizens lose their jobs. Free-marketeers Roger Kerr, Ron Trotter, Peter Shirtcliffe and Alan Gibbs speak gleefully of the model laissez-faire state, but the anxiety of New Zealanders who have been made redundant, or watched their local post office close forever tells a different story.

Treasury, home of the country's economic mandarins, comes across as the arch-villain, manipulating each new government with dire predictions, but equally sinister is the suggestion that academics are having their research funding cut if they speak out against the changes.

Stickmen

STICKMEN IS UNBASHEDLY a 'bloke's movie' in the genre of *Major League, Slap Shot* and *Cool Runnings.* Three lads hang out at Dave's Bar playing pool. The game provides an escape for each of them – Jack is oversexed, Wayne is undersexed, and Thomas doesn't know whether he is coming or going. (The film's title is an obvious Freudian pun.)

The three enter a pool competition organised by Daddy, the head of Wellington's Greek underworld. Besides fun, there is an

added incentive: Dave owes a bone-breaking amount to Daddy, and the prize pool will clear the debt and so save the lads' local.

This is not a profound or original movie. The scenario clearly has the caper films of Guy Ritchie (*Lock, Stock And Two Smoking Barrels, Snatch*) in its sights. There are hackneyed jokes, stereotypes in abundance, and the women characters are marginalised to the extent that every single one prostitutes herself one way or another. The contests are predictable – even the surprise twist happens right on cue.

However, *Stickmen* manages to be endearing and entertaining. Anne Nordhaus and Paolo Rotondo make a watchable couple worth caring about, Scott Wills is excellent as the sodden Wayne, and the variety of venues and opponents, from gay cowboys with screens of hardcore porn to distract the opposition to the disconcerting Men in Black, move the story along nicely. Helpfully, a Greek-chorus type character explains the rules of pub pool for those who don't understand unders, overs and the down-trou.

Stickmen
2001 / Feature / 93 mins

DIRECTOR / **Hamish Rothwell**
PRODUCER / **Michelle Turner**
SCREENPLAY / **Nick Ward**
PRODUCTION COMPANY / **Stick Films**

There is some snappy dialogue, and the slick production values bespeak the film-maker's career in advertising. Even so, the final shot uses a touch of number-8-wire technology: the eight-ball was suspended on a thread and the cast told to 'stand really still'.

Stickmen is itself like a game of pool. It gets on a roll at times, there are plot holes as big as the pockets, and it definitely improves after a beer or two.

Still Life

SIMA URALE'S DIRECTING DEBUT, *O Tamaiti,* was filmed entirely from the point of view of five Polynesian children: adults were large shadows, legs, and voices muffled by walls. In *Still Life* Urale goes to the other extreme: the world is experienced by elderly Europeans. The phone rings interminably as old limbs make their way along a corridor. Conversations are muffled as deafness intervenes. The outside world seems many miles away, happily ignoring an aged couple whose family is distant physically and emotionally.

There is a shadow over them – the wife is dying, and as she writhes in bed the love of her life feels every moment of her pain. Yet in the midst of this their intimacy thrives. He reads 'some of that Shakespeare bloke you like so much'. She smiles. 'I do so love to hear your voice.' It is one of the tenderest moments in New Zealand film.

Still Life, dealing deftly and sensitively with the subject of euthanasia, was a conscious attempt by Urale to show that she could empathise with non-Polynesian subject matter and she largely succeeds, although the respect and tenderness towards the elderly that she depicts is perhaps more typical of Samoan than palagi culture.

The complex sound design, the skilful cinematography that embraces the beauty in the actors' wrinkled skin, and the performances of the two leads, Joseph Hancox and June Bishop, are all notable. *Still Life* won the award for best short film at the 2001 Montreal Film Festival, and the following year also scored best director, best script and best art department at the Drifting Clouds International Film Festival in Wellington. And to show she was prepared to push into ever more diverse subject matter, Urale's next film, *Coffee And Allah*, was about a badminton-playing Muslim.

Still Life
2001 / Short / 12 mins

DIRECTOR / SCREENPLAY /
Sima Urale
PRODUCER / Anna Rasmussen
PRODUCTION COMPANY /
Niu Movies

Strike Zone

WITHOUT KNOWING ITS BACKGROUND, you could quibble as to whether *Strike Zone* deserves to be classified as an essential New Zealand film. There are many good things about it: it is strikingly edited, superbly acted, and the softball action sequences are imaginative and intimate – director Cameron Duncan managed to convince several members of the New Zealand softball team, the Black Sox, to appear, including the legendary Kevin Herlihy. However, the plot is squeezed too tightly into the short running time and parts of the film seem sophomoric. A feature film in the vein of *Remember The Titans* or *Hoosiers* is trying to burst out. No doubt lack of money and time constricted the narrative.

Time in particular, for Duncan (*DFK6498*), the seventeen-year-old Maori actor-director of *Strike Zone*, was dying of cancer. A secondary tumour in his lung burst while he was filming the softball sequence in the early hours of the morning. In a remarkable moment of sangfroid, Duncan depicted his own death and funeral on screen. He was quite disappointed at the attendance. 'It was a sad turnout,' he said, 'and I even provided pizza.'

Peter Jackson and Fran Walsh were among the people who recognised and nurtured Cameron Duncan's talent. Perhaps Jackson saw something of himself in the nascent but assured direction – in particular the war scenes, with their amateur pyrotechnics. Walsh movingly dedicated her 2003 Golden Globe for best original song ('Into the West') to the young director.

Within six months of filming, Duncan was dead. That in itself makes *Strike Zone* poignant, and the simple reflective lines that he delivers, sometimes with disarming humour, seem like weighty philosophical statements.

Strike Zone
2003 / Short / 10 mins

DIRECTOR / SCREENPLAY
Cameron Duncan
PRODUCTION COMPANY
Broadcast Arts

Even more poignant is to watch the handsome, charismatic young man and know the skill he possessed was never able to mature.

Sweetness

THE MAIN PROBLEM with experimental films is that, however interesting the journey, the experiments often fail. Films such as *Taunt* (Alison Maclean, 1983) and *Wog Features* (Lisa Reihana, 1990) toy with gender issues and sexuality, but don't hold together either as narrative or abstraction. *Rud's Wife* (Alison Maclean, 1985) and *Ashes* (Barry Barclay, 1975) play with the notion of

documentary without achieving verisimilitude. *Sweetness*, however, a single-shot film by Rachel Davies, not only deals with similar issues and stylistic challenges but also tells a story that is at once dramatic and emotionally complex.

Sweetness
1992 / Short / 9 mins

DIRECTOR / PRODUCER / SCREENPLAY / Rachel Davies

There are layers upon layers in this short. Davies' device of having a man's voice lip-synched by an androgynous woman (in fact Davies herself) blurs the line between genders, as well as between fiction and non-fiction. The story – the grooming and molestation of a boy scout – is told with hesitancy, simplicity and a quiet wit that seems too genuine to be invention.

Sweetness covers some of the territory that would later be traversed in Australian Mark Bellamy's short *A Lamb Of Our Own Flock* and Californian Gregg Araki's brilliant feature *Mysterious Skin* – the contradictory feelings of a boy who has had one of the most profound experiences of his life. The love the victim had for the Scout leader, and the heartbreak he felt when his abuser moved his attention to younger children, are compellingly presented.

After *Sweetness* picked up awards at the Sydney and San Francisco Film Festivals, Davies continued to make experimental short films, before moving into directing television commercials and music videos. With advent of Television on Demand in 2007, she became one of the makers of a new cultural programme, The Gravy, for TVNZ 6.

Sweetness is one of the few New Zealand shorts currently available on You Tube – an appropriately contemporary and accessible medium for such a successful experiment.

Take 3

IN RECENT YEARS several accomplished short films have reprised the experiences of first- and second-generation immigrants. Among them have been Sima Urale's *Coffee And Allah*, with its hypnotic blue chador, and Zia Mandviwalla's exquisitely constructed *Eating Sausage*.

Take 3
2008 / Short / 12 mins

DIRECTOR / SCREENPLAY / Roseanne Liang
PRODUCER / Owen Hughes
PRODUCTION COMPANY / Frame Up Films

And there has been strident Pacific Island cinema – occasionally dubbed Pollywood – including Miki Magasiva's *Uso*, Popo Lilo's *Tiga E Le Lloa*, and Justine Simei-Barton's *The Trophy*.

Take 3, by second-generation Chinese-New Zealander Roseanne Liang, is a tellingly comical look at the battles that people of Asian heritage have with stereotypes imposed by a European hegemony. Three young actresses seeking various roles at auditions are encouraged to be inscrutable, coquettish or martially artistic, before a final humiliation pushes the trio over the edge when they are urged to act like 'wartime Vietnamese hookers'.

Liang's first movie, *Banana In A Nutshell*, was an honest, intimate and funny documentary about the difficulties she faced trying to get her father's blessing to marry a European. She successfully transplants the same sense of humour into *Take 3*. Some of the scenes are cringingly funny, and the comic timing and deadpanning, particularly from Li Ming Hu, Katlyn Wong and Michelle Ang, are top-notch. There is witty use of split screens, and the final shot in which we follow each actress in a different direction is a bravura moment. The film received special mention at the Berlin Film Festival for its 'charismatic actresses and fresh approach'.

Talkback

LIKE ALL OF ALISON MACLEAN'S New Zealand films, *Talkback* is a psychological tour de force. The film opens with an American being interviewed, talking like a Gatling gun, insulting listeners, and opining freely and obnoxiously. This is confrontational radio – but soon the host, Roger (Alistair Douglas), is called away and Jonah (Lucy Sheehan), his producer and occasional lover, has to take over the broadcast.

With its plethora of characters, *Talkback* has something of the same flavour as Robert Altman's *Nashville*. Forced behind the microphone, Jonah enters into relationships with disembodied voices with names such as Waitangi Joe and Night Owl. As each caller talks we see their life in a short and striking tableau. The places they live, as portrayed by cinematographer Sally Bongers (*Sweetie*, *A Girl's Own Story*) and art director Jackie Gilmore (*An Angel At My Table*, *Jack Be Nimble*), are gritty and strangely impersonal – stark hotel rooms, sparse kitchens, tasteless interiors. Great use is made of Auckland's empty nocturnal landscape, including K Road's Uncle's Diner, and the famous White Lady pie cart.

Talkback's wordy script was developed by Maclean and Geoff Chapple after research on Radio Pacific. Issues that get an airing include indigenous rights, crime and the imperialism of the United States, but it is the tension between the sexes that really powers the drama. One recurring caller, an ex-con named Jim, both repels and attracts Jonah with his abrasiveness. The talented Peter Tait, later to play the beast in Maclean's *Kitchen Sink* (1989), has a similar role here: a man who initially seems feral, but may or may not be. The dialogue between Jim and Jonah sings with tension as Jonah feels both threatened and excited by the danger.

Talkback
1987 Feature 50 mins
DIRECTOR SCREENPLAY **Alison Maclean**
PRODUCER **Bridget Ikin**
PRODUCTION COMPANY **Hibiscus Films**

The ending avoids easy resolutions. Jonah strides confidently away from the studio, but there is a pervading melancholy: a night of mystery and intimacy has dissipated with the dawn.

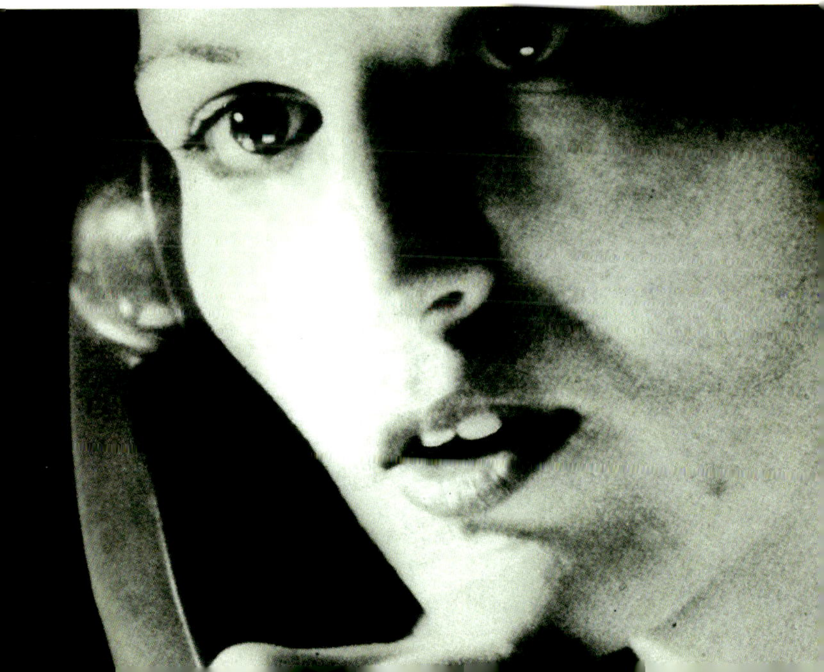

Tama Tu

TAMA TU'S ALMOST WORDLESS SCRIPT very skilfully conveys camaraderie, wit, poignancy and humanity in the midst of war. That all six characters manage to be convincing and emerge as individuals is remarkable for so short a film.

It is Italy 1944, and members of the 28th Maori Battalion of the New Zealand Expeditionary Force are involved in urban warfare. As night approaches they hole up in a ruined house. With a watch in place they relax, but not completely.

Director Taika Waititi (*Eagle vs Shark, Two Cars, One Night*) shows he is the master of comic timing: the physical comedy from Jarod Rawiri and Mark Ruka is a memorable reminder that these men in khaki who are willing to ask their brothers in arms to 'pull their fingers' are also young, bawdy and silly.

Yet there are other things going on beyond the fart jokes and pulled faces. When one of the men finds a tin soldier, there is splendid irony as he mimics explosions around it. When the lookout (Emile Taungaroa) spies a German soldier he lines up his rifle to snipe him, but seeing that the man is reaching out to stroke a cat he lowers his gun – empathising with another soldier seeking an escape from war in something banal and normal. Set a time when both were in short supply, *Tama Tu* finds humour and compassion in the most unlikely of settings.

Tama Tu

2004 / Short / 17 mins

DIRECTOR / SCREENPLAY / Taika Waititi

PRODUCERS / Ainsley Gardiner, Cliff Curtis

PRODUCTION COMPANY / Aio Films/Defender Films

The Te Kooti Trail

BORN IN 1900, RUDALL HAYWARD directed four feature films before he turned thirty. Two of them, *Rewi's Last Stand* and *The Te Kooti Trail*, are among the most assured features ever made in New Zealand.

Hayward's position at the vanguard of New Zealand cinema should have elevated his reputation to that of his famous contemporaries such as rugby's George Nepia, literature's Frank Sargeson and aviation's Jean Batten. That he is less famous is largely because much of his work was lost as the nitrate decayed.

In addition, Hayward's abilities declined. The sound version of *Rewi's Last Stand*, released in 1940 and ironically Hayward's best known film, is both overly melodramatic and lacks the balanced portrayal of opposing sides that Hayward had achieved in his first version. His last feature, *To Love A Maori*, shows a lack of basic technical skills to match the earnest storyline.

Following Hayward's great burst of activity in the 1920s – as well as the four features, he made over thirty short films – his output dropped dramatically. Nevertheless, what he achieved at such a young age is remarkable. The silent version of *Rewi's Last Stand* is one of the sad palimpsests of New Zealand cinema. The thirty minutes that still exist suggest both emotional complexity and a narrative far ahead of its time. The capture by a Maori war party of the lead character, a British soldier attached to von Tempsky's

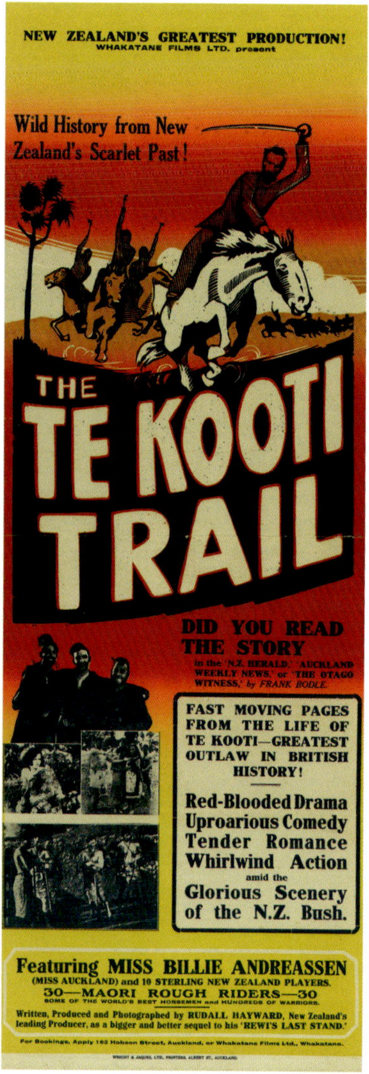

Forest Rangers, allows a view behind 'enemy' lines, rather than just a colonial perspective, and the Maori warriors are portrayed as doggedly heroic.

The Te Kooti Trail has similar two-sidedness, although the overall tone is an apologia for colonialism and integration, and the intertitles underscore the idea that European settlement is beneficial for Maori.

The bulk of the narrative is based on an 1869 incident in which a small settlement near Whakatane was overwhelmed by forces led by Te Kooti, a Maori leader and anti-colonial guerilla. Identification with and sympathy for the colonials is obvious: Geoffrey Mantell was a disgraced military officer in England, but here he is part of an honourable 'legion' working with Lieutenant Gilbert Mair to protect settlers.

Hayward strove for historical accuracy, even consulting an elderly Mair. He deals carefully with the complex figure of Te Kooti, suggesting much of his movement's brutality emanated from his lieutenant, 'half-caste' Baker McLean, and accepting Te Kooti's rejection of orthodox Christianity in favour of the Ringatu faith he founded. Even so, Te Kooti's grim camp in the mountains of the Urewera is contrasted with the bucolic, jolly Mill Farm, where Frenchman Jean Guerrin (H. Redmond) operates a flour mill.

The Te Kooti Trail
1927 / Feature / 103 mins

DIRECTOR / PRODUCER / **Rudall Hayward**
SCREENPLAY / **Rudall Hayward, Frank Bodle**
PRODUCTION COMPANY / **Whakatane Films**

Guerrin has wed a Maori woman in what must be one of the first onscreen interracial marriages in the world (and, more importantly, one not subject to any directorial comment). There is other romance as well – Guerrin's wife's sister Monika (played with effervescence by Tina Hunt), enjoys a romantic, beautifully filmed canoe ride with her beau, Taranahi (Peter Warbrick). However, this Arcadian life is interrupted by Te Kooti's raiding party. Highlights include a tracking shot of Te Kooti's men advancing towards the redoubt, and long shots of Mair (Thomas McDermott) desperately riding to Tauranga for reinforcements.

As with many of Hayward's films, *The Te Kooti Trail* is a clumsy and sometimes disconcerting mix of romance, action and comedy, marred by some overacting. However, it is also a considered examination of the relationship between pakeha and Maori, a theme that would abide in Rudall Hayward's work until his death in 1974.

This Is New Zealand

THIS IS NEW ZEALAND was a triumphant accomplishment by the National Film Unit. Commissioned for the New Zealand Pavilion at Expo '70 in Osaka, Japan, it was widely regarded as the best of the one hundred films there. The aerial shots of the Southern Alps, filmed with three cameras squeezed into the nose of a plane and accompanied by Sibelius's stirring 'Karelia Suite', are among the most famous scenes in New Zealand cinema history.

Conceived to fill a massive three-part screen – wide enough to capture New Zealand's broad panoramas – *This Is New Zealand* was made with three 35-millimetre cameras working synchronously, and needed 70 tonnes of equipment to project. The triple screen had been used before – most notably in Abel Gance's 1927 epic *Napoléon* – but the project was still spectacularly ambitious.

This was not to be simply an oversize moving postcard. It had to tell the story of the country and its people. The script was carefully developed to incorporate symmetrical shots, and multiple images related through subject or movement. The juxtapositions lent themselves to visual puns: a cattle beast on one screen becomes a steak on the next; a pneumatic drill morphs into a dentist at work.

This Is New Zealand
1970 / Short / 19 mins

DIRECTOR / Hugh MacDonald
PRODUCTION COMPANY / New Zealand National Film Unit

Today the film is a nostalgia trip through life in the early '70s, from walk shorts and dress socks to newly fashionable mini-skirts. There is spectacular footage from a racing car, and a well-shot cattle round-up at Molesworth Station. New Zealanders mow their lawns, watch sport and attend their local A&P show. An enormous logging truck roars across all three screens, and a deer trots sedately.

The rhythm of the editing is breathtaking, following long sweeps over landscape with so many images the eye can barely keep up. The music includes incidental passages from The Avengers and the Hamilton County Bluegrass Band.

Over two million people experienced *This Is New Zealand* in Japan and another 350,000 in New Zealand, where it played three times an hour in the biggest theatres in the main centres. The film moved many New Zealanders, including politicians, to tears. After a government screening, the hard-boiled minister of finance (and later prime minister) Robert Muldoon was told the film had been made within budget. He gruntily replied: 'I wouldn't have cared if it had cost double.'

86

Tongan Ninja

THIS PARODY OF MARTIAL ARTS MOVIES oscillates between gusset-tearingly funny and weepingly silly. *Tongan Ninja* makes a bold statement – why spend hundreds of millions of dollars on a bunch of Orcs and Ringwraiths when across town you can make a great movie – with ninjas! – for $3.40 and an empty packet of Snifters. The film doesn't just have contempt for 'high' production values, it wags its butt and makes donkey noises at them. Never before has a boom mike been so visible, and so very useful.

The lead character, both Tongan and a ninja, comes to New Zealand to save an oriental eatery from falling into the hands of the So Called Syndicate. In time he falls in love with sultry Miss Lee, defeats Knife Man, Gun Man and Asian Sidekick, and faces his nemesis, Action Fighter; his tactics are the pink hand, irritating poke, and bite of the horse. His chest hair proves to be his Achilles heel.

As its publicity material suggests, *Tongan Ninja* was 'shot in stunning yet convenient locations'. Great and occasionally illegal use was made of Wellington landmarks such as the Mount Victoria bus tunnel, the Karori Wildlife Sanctuary, the Massey Memorial (Action Fighter's Patio of Death), and the dog-and-master statue at the bottom of Plimmer Steps.

It also features 'exciting new sound and special effects techniques designed to fool the extremely gullible into thinking it was done for real'. There are sight gags all over the place, and the hilarious throwaway asides of Dave Fane (Herman the Henchman) and the ninjas make it worthwhile keeping your finger waggling above the rewind button. There are cameos from Taika Waititi as a break-dancing chef, Jed Brophy as a bank manager, and Tana Umaga as a famous rugby player. Linda Tseng sizzles as Miss Lee, not that Tongan Ninja notices. As Action Fighter, Jemaine Clement (*Eagle vs Shark*, *Fizz*) puts the 'abs' into 'absurd' and provides the overdubbed taunts exchanged by Mr Fighter and the Tongan Ninja. He also sings the addictive theme song. Appalling overdubbing means lip-readers will enjoy a completely different movie.

Tongan Ninja
2002 / Feature / 82 mins

DIRECTOR / Jason Stutter
PRODUCERS / Andrew Calder, Jason Stutter
SCREENPLAY / Jason Stutter, Jemaine Clement
PRODUCTION COMPANY / Tommy Ringo International

Topless Women Talk About Their Lives

OCCASIONALLY THE HARSH REALITIES of making a movie in New Zealand clash with persistent genius. Such was the case with *Topless Women Talk About Their Lives*, a film that shouldn't exist. It does so only because the director and a couple of actors wanted it to, and had a few free weekends.

In spite of his wonderfully circular Front Lawn comedies *Walk-short*, *The Lounge Bar* and *Linda's Body*, Harry Sinclair encountered problems when he tried to get accepted as a serious contender to direct a longer work. In response, he and some actor friends conceived a mini soap opera of three-minute episodes to screen between programmes on late-night television. The series was largely improvised, with the story being made up as they went along. After twelve episodes, Sinclair approached the New Zealand Film Commission with a good portion of a feature film already complete – and finally received some funding.

Topless Women is fuelled by the joy of making a movie under severe financial restrictions. Each day's script was written the night before it was shot, and ideas were workshopped as they were filmed, lending a naturalness to the dialogue and immediacy to every scene. The film deals with the important stuff of contemporary life – lust, love, marriage, pregnancy, mental illness, commitment and career. Danielle Cormack's real-life pregnancy was incorporated into the story.

The downside of the methodology is that the narrative is disjointed. After opening with a joke about *The Piano*, it oscillates from candid realism to joyous stupidity, and for a while shifts into disconcertingly dark territory.

Topless Women Talk About Their Lives
1997 / Feature / 89 mins

DIRECTOR / SCREENPLAY / Harry Sinclair
PRODUCERS / Fiona Copland, Harry Sinclair
PRODUCTION COMPANY / John Swimmer Productions

Overall, though, this is a pacy urban comedy about a quite dysfunctional bunch of twenty-something friends. Ant the film-maker is an absurd Chaplinesque character upon whom many humiliations are heaped, not least the writing of a terrible film called *Topless Women…* Danielle Cormack is luminous as the unexpectedly expectant mother. Flying Nun's outstanding soundtrack features classic songs from the 3Ds, the Chills, the Clean and the Bats.

The Topp Twins: Untouchable Girls

SOMEWHERE IN THE MIDDLE OF THIS FILM the personal story of Jools and Lynda Topp transforms into a history of protest movements – Bastion Point, the 1981 Springbok Tour, homosexual law reform, the anti-nuclear movement, the fight for free breast cancer medication. These events may have seemed oblique were it not for the fact that the Topp Twins were at the heart of them all – sabotaging proposed Bastion Point housing developments with concrete, standing in the thick of protesters at Hamilton's Rugby Park, sporting electric pink on the Herceptin Heroines rally.

Luckily there is enough in interviews with their fabulous parents and partners, the heartbreaking video of Jools' chemotherapy and the Topps' own commentary to uncover the girls behind the gingham. Director Leanne Pooley's great skill as a magpie means we are also treated to hilarious television reporting, some priceless snaps, and memorable footage from concerts and protests.

For much of its length this is a performance film: a cabaret act in front of celebrities and friends (including Helen Clark, John Clarke, Billy Bragg and Don McGlashan) provides a frame for the biographies. However, this seems tame compared to the kinetic material: the twins busking on Queen Street, touring the country in a tractor-drawn gypsy caravan, hamming it up backstage in the Wanganui Opera House, performing in a packed marquee at an Australian folk festival. In such scenes the Topps display their ability both to improvise and to enrapture an audience with anarchy and absurdity.

The Topps have genuine affection for their Kiwiana caricatures. There are delightful scenes where their most famous characters – Ken and Ken, the Bowling Ladies, Camp Leader and Camp Mother, and Prue and Dilly – talk about the twins before the twins talk about them. This is not the comedy of cruelty but a heartwarming tribute to New Zealand and its odd and charming personalities, and the humour to be found in horn-rimmed spectacles and lamingtons.

The Topp Twins: Untouchable Girls
2009 / Documentary / 85 mins

DIRECTOR / WRITER / **Leanne Pooley**
PRODUCER / **Arani Cuthbert**
PRODUCTION COMPANY / **Diva Productions**

Turangawaewae/ A Place To Stand

WHEN WI KUKI KAA DIED IN 2005 at the age of sixty-seven, he had been at the pinnacle of Maori acting for the best part of twenty-five years, whether as the station manager in *Ngati*, the tattooist-chief in *River Queen*, or the flatulent free spirit in *Thunderbox*. A versatile performer, he had also taken on television roles as diverse as the travelling scarecrow maker in *Worzel Gummidge* and Nikolu Yaramoto in *Spyforce*.

One of Kaa's great performances is in *Turangawaewae*, a beautifully realised short film by Peter Burger (*The Tattooist, Fish Skin Suit*). Kaa plays Tiare, a homeless man haunted by the trauma and guilt he experienced as a soldier in the Vietnam War, and suffering the effects of age. Cantankerous and unbalanced, he refuses the attempts of his daughter (Nancy Brunning) to take him back to his home marae, preferring to live in a shelter for the homeless. His improvised turangawaewae, his 'home', is a piece of turf stolen from a bowling club.

After a spectacularly realistic accident on Wellington's Lambton Quay, Tiare's mental, physical and, most importantly, spiritual health become so fragile that his daughter and mokopuna manage to return him to his ancestral hearth. He takes off his shoes and socks and his toes finally dig into his true turangawaewae. His healing can begin.

This uplifting film written by Wiremu Grace was inspired by

his grandfather's experiences in the 28th Maori Battalion in the Second World War. It includes a superb scene where a gang member buys Tiare something to eat, and cameos from Taika Waititi and Grant Tilly. Warren Maxwell of Trinity Roots provides the closing song, 'Little Things'. *Turangawaewae/A Place To Stand* was selected for Critics' Week at the Cannes Film Festival.

Turangawaewae/ A Place To Stand
2003 Short 13 mins

DIRECTOR Peter Burger
PRODUCER Catherine Fitzgerald
SCREENPLAY Wiremu Grace
PRODUCTION COMPANY Blueskin Films

Two Cars, One Night

MUCH OF TAIKA WAITITI'S CAREER has involved visual jokes and slapstick, so a gentle comedy about kids seems altogether out of character. That he achieves a funny, touching romance set in the wasteland of child neglect shows his remarkable directorial skill.

Two Cars, One Night won plaudits and prizes at many international film festivals, and deservedly attracted an Academy Award nomination for best live action short; at the Oscar ceremony in the famed Kodak Theatre in Los Angeles, Waititi snaffled media attention by feigning sleep.

The plot of *Two Cars, One Night* is simple. Two boys are left in their parents' car outside a pub. Romeo is bored; his brother Ed, who is probably 'one of them gays', sits reading. When a young girl's parents pull up and leave her in the car park too, Romeo belies his name. 'Hey, Ugly,' he taunts.

Even in such a limited space, Waititi finds visual comedy – Romeo plays amusingly with the carseat recliner, and his facial expressions reveal a comic genius in the making – but the contact between Polly and Romeo, enhanced by black and white photography, is thoroughly realistic. Stylistic touches such as lighted cigarettes tracing patterns like sparklers, and clouds whipping by show how slowly time is passing, but once Polly sees through Romeo's braggadocio his attentions relieve the tedium. When a 'diamond' ring is exchanged, first love coalesces.

This quasi-adult affection between such young characters – Romeo is nine, Polly eleven – and in such unpromising circumstances convinces largely because of the exquisite performances. The three children, Rangi Ngamoki, Hutini Waikato and Te Ahiwaru Ngamoki-Richards, were all untrained actors, discovered at a school near Te Kaha where the film is set, and coached by actor Nancy Brunning. The script helps by eschewing triteness: the kids speak in believable patois.

Two Cars, One Night
2003 / Short / 11 mins

DIRECTOR / SCREENPLAY / Taika Waititi
PRODUCERS / Ainsley Gardiner, Catherine Fitzgerald
PRODUCTION COMPANY / Defender Films

Taiko Waititi's first feature film, *Eagle vs Shark* (2007), saw him swing back to absurd physical comedy, but his second, provisionally titled *Volcano*, promises to return to Te Kaha and expand on this sweet, funny and uplifting short.

Utu

'WHEN YOU MAKE A FILM ABOUT RACIAL CONFLICT, you are living dangerously,' Geoff Murphy said. 'When you make a film about racial conflict in a country that congratulates itself on what a successful bicultural society it is, the danger heightens.'

His point was well-taken. When *Utu* was released, it was flamed by local critics as a 'Puha western'. Murphy was said to have borrowed the style of Sergio Leone and John Ford, replacing Native Americans with Maori, and United States cavalrymen with red-coated, pith-helmeted British soldiers.

This was, of course, partially true – and not unusual: the western genre often tells stories from the serrated edge of colonisation, where settlers encounter indigenous people with unease and violence. Other films dealing with the subject – for example, *Zulu* (South Africa), *The Story Of The Kelly Gang*, *The Phantom Stockman*, *The Proposition* and *Australia* (Australia) and *Black God, White Devil* (Brazil) – have also borrowed the language of the western. Rudall Hayward's 1927 *The Te Kooti Trail* used elements of early westerns such as *Gunslinger* and *The Great Train Robbery*.

And sure, there is a saloon shooting, a wagon hold-up, and a man in a wide-brimmed hat. But to dismiss *Utu* as a western knock-off is to ignore the intelligent script by Keith Aberdein, the anarchic tone – this was, after all, Murphy's follow-up to *Goodbye Pork Pie* – and a perspective that shifts between settlers and tangata whenua.

Utu
1983 / Feature / 116 mins

DIRECTOR / PRODUCER /
Geoff Murphy
SCREENPLAY / Keith Aberdein, Geoff Murphy

The main character, Te Wheke, is an amalgam of historic Maori leaders Te Kooti, Wiremu Tamihana, Kereopa Te Rau and Te Rauparaha. A scout for the colonial forces during the New Zealand Wars, he rebels and seeks utu – revenge – when his home village is sacked. His taking of ta moko is the most visible mark of his rejection of colonial values, and gives New Zealand cinema one of its great faces. As Te Wheke, Anzac Wallace oscillates between nobility and savagery, and sympathy for him is regularly undercut by his violent eruptions.

There are some fantastic moments, among them Te Wheke quoting *Macbeth* as his warriors camouflage themselves, a suspenseful church confrontation, and a chilling scene when Te Wheke holds his hand next to that of a European before killing him and going berserk. There is also some disarming gallows humour, and notable performances from Ilona Rogers, Bruno Lawrence, and Wi Kuki Kaa as Wiremu, the 'friendly' Maori.

At the climactic trial each person who has been offended against argues as to why they should exact utu and kill Te Wheke. Wiremu projects a possible future of compromise and shared understanding, but this is no facile solution: a convert to Christianity, he says a prayer to the rifle he is about to use to do the deed. This fratricidal moment is almost Shakespearean in its emotional complexity.

Utu was made on an epic scale, with local Maori consulted and employed, the full New Zealand Symphony Orchestra playing the score, and a steadicam used for battle scenes – a New Zealand first.

A Very Nice Honeymoon

THE SIMMONDS BROTHERS specialise in 'documation', recording unscripted audio and marrying it to animated cartoon characters. Using this method, they have made such charming films as *Pearl, Florrie And The Bull* (a true story of eighty-year-old twin sisters being attacked by livestock), *The Wedding Speech* and *Paekakariki: The Centre Of The Universe.*

Their most personal film, however, has been the story of their great-grandparents' journey from Dalmatia. Mariano and Elizabeth Vella were shipwrecked on Great Barrier Island in 1894, when the SS *Wairarapa* foundered with 131 people lost. It was the couple's honeymoon.

A Very Nice Honeymoon
2006 / Short / 10 mins

DIRECTORS / PRODUCERS / SCREENPLAY / Jeff Simmonds, Phill Simmonds
PRODUCTION COMPANY / Simmonds Brothers

The story has the status of myth within the Simmonds family. The brothers used tape recordings made by Elizabeth in the 1950s describing the wreck and her survival, and by her daughter, Metty, retelling her version of events in 1986. Contemporary recordings were made of their uncle and mother, the brothers themselves, and Elizabeth's great-great-grandchild Rachel telling the story to a primary-school class. This gives the narrative a Chinese whispers' feel, with each generation stressing different aspects of the story.

In spite of the tragedy depicted, this is an endearing sliver of family history, and there is humour as characters bicker, interrupt and correct each other in the way only families can. Geoff Duncan's haunting score was inspired by four chords played randomly on an autoharp by Phill Simmonds.

Vigil

VIGIL IS PERHAPS THE MOST 'EUROPEAN' MOVIE made in New Zealand to date: amid the shearing shed, docking of lambs and red-band gumboots, it has the slow, grim beauty of Andrei Tarkovsky or Ingmar Bergman. Vincent Ward's eye for mise en scène gives *Vigil* much of its haunting quality. Images remain long after the credits roll: the young girl Toss with a balaclava and totem; a branch blowing away in a squall; mourners in their weeds huddling before a newly filled grave; the tracking shot as Toss hurtles down a ridge.

In preparation for *Vigil*, Ward spent many days at New York's Museum of Modern Art watching silent films. The result was a belief in the ability of strong images to convey a profound and difficult story. The dialogue in *Vigil* is spare, but the relationships between the characters are complicated and intense.

On the surface *Vigil* is simple. Like all of Ward's work it depicts people struggling with their landscape. Four people live in a swampy valley, where 'we can't stop the hills caving in on us'. If the raw hills are forbidding the farmhouse is worse, offering no warmth except biblical picture books. Just as Ward finds poetry in a colloquial setting, there are suggestions of previous, less primitive lives – Toss's mother Elizabeth, for example, has been a ballerina – but this is subsumed by the settler myth of breaking the rugged land, or it breaking the characters.

The landscape literally takes Toss's father; he is killed trying to rescue a sheep. In the grim surroundings, his young daughter puts together fragments of reality, sieved through her fantasia, in an attempt to make sense of her father's death and her mother's relationship with a poacher, Ethan.

Initially, Toss sees Ethan as an Old Testament devil who must be expelled from the valley. Later she befriends him when he seems to be able to perform magic; together they give God a small offering of Wattie's baked beans. But when a sexual relationship begins between Ethan and her mother, Toss retreats to her grandfather's hut, where most of the communication with the outside world is through blasts of a tuba.

While there are only five characters in this film, many things seem to come alive – the bizarre piece of drilling machinery built by Ethan and the grandfather, Birdie; the tractor that chugs to its demise in a pond; the hills that shrug the father to his death. In Toss's haunting dream, electric shears dance wildly.

Vigil
1984 / Feature / 90 mins

DIRECTOR / Vincent Ward
PRODUCER / John Maynard
SCREENPLAY / Vincent Ward, Graham Tetley, Fiona Lindsay
PRODUCTION COMPANY / John Maynard Productions

The film's cinematographer, Alun Bollinger, uses an almost monochromatic palette: everything is dull green and brown. The occasional intrusion of bright colours such as Toss's pink tutu or the blood on her face is startling. Alongside this, the eerie sounds of the valley – banshee winds, bird calls, and echoed booms of firearms – are accentuated and distorted to depict Toss's reality. Jack Body's score is stark and unsettling.

The professionals do well – Frank Whitten as the poacher is both ominous and human – but it is the schoolgirl Fiona Kay who sets the standard. In his meticulous preparation, Ward sorted through images of around 40,000 schoolgirls before seeing in Kay something of himself. The young star excels at depicting confusion (as she menstruates for the first time), devotion (in her shrine to her lost father), and a vivid imagination created by the loneliness of isolation, which for Ward was semi-autobiographical.

Vigil is an art film and may be too slow and interior for many tastes, but it was an early triumph of art cinema in New Zealand. The first local feature film to be selected to screen in Competition at the Cannes Film Festival, it was subsequently released on screens around the world.

The Waimate Conspiracy

IN THE 1920S RUDALL HAYWARD travelled the length and breadth of the country, making and screening community features with names such as *Winifred Of Wanganui, Patsy Of Palmerston* and *A Daughter Of Wairoa*. Local identities played roles alongside professional actors, and ordinary folk took the minor parts. Soon after filming, the features would be screened for an eager audience.

If Hayward were alive today, he might be carrying a digital video camera and making a rollicking comedy like *The Waimate Conspiracy*. There is something gloriously amateur about the whole affair – the South Canterbury town contributed its mayor, police chief and even a landlady to play themselves – but there is also something captivating.

The plot revolves around efforts by local Maori to lay a land claim, and the difficulties they face when evidence keeps being destroyed – until they decide to manufacture some of their own. The potentially controversial subject matter and deeply felt emotions are never allowed to swamp the light humour. The head of the claimant family, George Kepa (Jim Moriarty), may be powered by passion, but he is charming and vivid and funny.

In keeping with the amiable story, the characters are not played for laughs, except for the inept cameraman Dave, whom we never see but who contributes enough crashes and poor panning to provide a decent cover for the speed of filming and

The Waimate Conspiracy
2006 / Feature / 101 mins

DIRECTOR / PRODUCER / SCREENPLAY / **Stefen Lewis**
PRODUCTION COMPANY / **Dark Horse Productions**

inevitable errors. More than once you sense that Jim Moriarty is directing the shot from in front of the lens as he tells Dave to shift.

The real-life Dave – Stefen Lewis, who also wrote the novel on which the film is based – was interested in film from an early age; in the 1970s he came second in a *Spot On* competition, behind a film about a Cyclops by a kid called Peter Jackson. But whereas Jackson became an Oscar winner, when Lewis made *The Waimate Conspiracy* he was working as a community policeman in Christchurch.

This film wasn't even made on a shoestring – rather the little plastic bit at the end. The veteran comic David McPhail was paid in petrol vouchers for his role as a judge, and Mark Hadlow and Helen Pearse-Otene bolstered the cast. However, the real charm is in the volunteers, who almost universally put in excellent turns.

This is an endearing effort that never tries to hide the fact that the cast and crew were working mostly for kai and the satisfaction of the final product. *The Waimate Conspiracy* won best film at several film festivals in New Zealand and overseas, and best digital film in the 2007 Air New Zealand Screen Awards. Not bad for six days' work.

Walkshort

WALKSHORT RESEMBLES Robert Altman's *Short Cuts*, but shorter and funnier and without Huey Lewis. A witty circular film by multimedia group the Front Lawn – Harry Sinclair (*Braindead, Linda's Body*) and Don McGlashan (*Drum/Sing, Linda's Body*) – its characters bump into each other, sometimes literally, as they walk down Auckland's Karangahape Road. In a structure à la *La Ronde* or a medley relay, the characters give short snapshots of their live direct to camera as they walk, until the next accidental encounter.

This is an examination of the glue that binds society – or doesn't: the transitions between one character and the next, apart from the first and last, are almost all misunderstandings.

The first character we meet is feeling great. The rash on his neck has cleared up, and he's smiling so much people probably think he has come into money, or just had really great sex. But then someone comes up and kicks him in the shin. A man in dress socks and walk shorts comes to his aid. He is shocked at the random violence but worried that assisting the man will make him late. He buys a bandage from a chemist, who in turn frets that he is too abrupt with customers … and so on, and on. The developer who tells us he's going to be putting up 'some pretty ugly buildings, cheaply made' that are 'just a speculation' is followed by German tourists in tapa shirts having a great day – until they realise they are lost.

All of the film's bewildering range of characters are played by either Sinclair or McGlashan, sometimes both together. There are misanthropes and homophobes, strangers who make innocuous threats, and old friends who suffer awkward silences. The hilarious soundtrack is composed of car horns and jackhammers, doors slamming and footsteps. The shop window credits are the icing on the doughnut. The entire film took just one day to shoot.

Walkshort
1988 / Short / 10 mins

DIRECTOR / SCREENPLAY / **William Toepfer**
PRODUCER / **Gregory Rood**
PRODUCTION COMPANY / **Front Lawn Films**

War Stories Our Mothers Never Told Us

THE BEST FILM AT THE 1995 New Zealand Film and Television Awards was a documentary that relied principally on talking-head interviews with seven elderly women. The film has no visual pyrotechnics, and only an occasional photograph, document, Pathé newsreel and *Weekly Review* clip to fill in the background. That it is so seductive is a tribute to the women, and the stories that they finally got to tell.

War Stories began as an idea during Gaylene Preston's research for *Bread And Roses*, her 1993 biopic of veteran trade unionist Sonja Davies. That film, like *Sands Of Iwo Jima, Embers, Dead Letters, Absent Without Leave* and *The Last Tattoo*, canvassed the years during the Second World War when the nation's men enlisted and went to overseas theatres of war, and women entered the industrial workforce and took other roles previously barred by patriarchal structures.

War Stories provides a factual fillip to those features. Seven women, one of whom died before the film screened, tell of losing husbands and fiancés, having extramarital affairs, including romances with American GIs, and in one case enduring ostracism as the wife of a conscientious objector. The director's approach is hands-off: there is minimal soundtrack, and interruptions by the interviewer, Judith Fyfe, are rare.

The most stunning aspect is the women's honesty and candour

as they speak of sex, grief, verbal abuse, and most especially love. Their colloquial and remarkably prosaic descriptions of momentous events have great power, and there are some amazing revelations – the drowning of American servicemen off Mana Island, a gang rape during active service, and, perhaps most movingly, the admission by Gaylene Preston's own mother, Tui, of her love for someone other than her husband.

War Stories Our Mothers Never Told Us
1995 / Documentary / 90 mins

DIRECTOR / PRODUCER / WRITER
Gaylene Preston

PRODUCTION COMPANY
Gaylene Preston Productions

Whale Rider

FROM THE TERRIBLE OPENING SCENE, where Pai is born while her mother and twin brother die, this is a film bearing strong emotions. In the hands of less assured talent than Niki Caro it could have been overwrought or hackneyed, but there is nothing in *Whale Rider* that is taken for granted, least of all the audience.

Caro has a strong feminist vision. Most of her fiction films (with the obvious exception of *Old Bastards*) depict women and their efforts at empowerment. In *Sure To Rise* the main character, beachcomber April, defies authority and gravity; in *The Summer The Queen Came* the mother, Hannah, is a political activist; in *Memory And Desire* Sayo strides away from traditional life as a widow.

Caro takes the novel by Witi Ihimaera and makes Pai the narrator, focussing on her relationship with her beloved and belligerent grandfather. Koro adores Pai – doubling her proudly to school on a bike – but he curses her gender and the lack of a male heir to lead the tribe. Secretly, Pai challenges Maori tikanga and learns some of the chiefly, exclusively male, skills to claim the birthright that comes with her name.

Ironically, Niki Caro faced a similar situation to Pai's, but it was her race, rather than her gender, that was the problem for her in being accepted as the appropriate teller of this Ngati Konohi story. There were meetings with elders. An adviser was to be on the set at all times. Caro learned te reo, and prayers were said regularly

to ward off bad luck that might have attached to the breaches of tikanga – such as Pai, a girl, learning the taiaha – that were needed for the tale to be told.

Whale Rider was largely filmed on location at Whangara on the east coast, giving it a powerful sense of place, and seeming to invoke the wairua of the iwi. The cast is almost exclusively Maori, with many of the supporting cast coming from the tangata whenua. The film's pace is rhythmic like the sea, an omnipresent force.

The cinematography of Leon Narbey is lyrical, the score by Lisa Gerrard conjures emotion, and the special effects, particularly the complex whale models, convince.

This straightforward story needed top-class performances and there is no disappointment here: Cliff Curtis, Rawiri Paratene, Manu Taumaunu and Grant Roa are especially good. And then there is the performance of Keisha Castle-Hughes, in an awe-

Whale Rider
2002 / Feature / 97 mins

DIRECTOR / SCREENPLAY / Niki Caro
PRODUCERS / Tim Sanders, John Barnett, Frank Hubner
PRODUCTION COMPANY / South Pacific Pictures

inspiring role for any actor, let alone one not yet in her teens. Only the most stoic could avoid being moved by Pai's sad but defiant speech of tribute to her absent Koro.

Whale Rider became an international success on the back of these qualities. It made US$21 million at the American box office, a figure for a New Zealand film surpassed to date only by Peter Jackson's *Lord Of The Rings* trilogy and *King Kong*. The film's themes of self-determination and a culture trying to reconcile traditional practices with modern realities resonated with audiences everywhere.

Why Can't I Stop This Uncontrollable Dancing?

WORKING IN A VIDEO STORE is almost a rite of passage for an aspiring director. Campbell Walker passed his days in Wellington's Aro Video absorbing the films of John Cassavetes, the Dardenne brothers and Andrei Tarkovsky. Perhaps as a result, his films have an intimacy and banality that make them defiantly uncommercial.

Why Can't I Stop This Uncontrollable Dancing?, a feature filmed on digital video, would probably never have received funding for celluloid, even if Walker had wanted it. The film is too small, too close and too cathartic to be commercially successful. And there is just the baldest rune of a narrative.

Leah lives in an Aro Valley flat. Waking with a hangover, she finds eighteen new messages on her phone from Terry, a fervent ex-boyfriend. As she sits in the bath and listens to them, her anxiety grows. When Terry reveals he is hitchhiking to Wellington and is already halfway there, the air is suddenly full of menace. When he eventually arrives there is an awkward stand-off on the porch. Terry walks away punching a letter box and Leah repeatedly impales a banana with a pen. In the film's minimalist landscape, these actions are mountainous and shocking.

Without the sublime acting of Nia Robyn this film would not have worked. Robyn's relationship with the movie camera has been

Why Can't I Stop This Uncontrollable Dancing?
2003 / Feature / 109 mins

DIRECTOR / SCREENPLAY / **Campbell Walker**
PRODUCERS / **Campbell Walker, Diane McAllen**
PRODUCTION COMPANY / **Gordon Productions**

described as a pas de deux: the camera loves Robyn's beauty, and she seems both attracted and repelled by the camera's presence. As emotions flicker over her face the audience becomes voyeuristic: we too are stalking Leah.

Digital film has opened up new ways of telling a story and this largely improvised film is a perfect example. Hyper-long shots allow scenes to beat to a weekend's languorous rhythms, and long pauses and inaction ratchet up the intensity. Shot with natural light, hand-held camera and diegetic soundtrack, *Uncontrollable Dancing* and companion Aro Valley pieces are as close to the Danish Dogme 95 movement as have been made in New Zealand.

Woodenhead

A UNIQUE ENTRY to New Zealand cinema history, *Woodenhead* – part musical, part road movie and wholly weird – is also strangely beguiling. The audio was recorded before the film was shot, and the visuals were then made to match (or not, as is often the case). The effect is dream-like: the actors seem to perform completely independently of their voices.

This unusual production technique was apparently inspired by a dream that director Florian Habicht had about the infamous lip-synching pop duo Milli Vanilli. It allowed him to cast actors purely for their looks. Leading man Nicholas Butler, who has an astoundingly unusual face, plays dump-hand Gert, while Teresa Peters plays Princess Plum, and also the Circus Dog.

Habicht was born in Germany, grew up in Northland, and has clearly seen David Lynch movies. This mélange of influences is clear: the donkey, surnames and burlesque are Teutonic; the tui, bellbirds and pie cart obviously New Zealand. The dance Plum and Gert share is a companion piece to the dwarf's dance in *Twin Peaks*. Every second character seems like an extra from *Eraserhead* – or perhaps *Little Red Riding Hood*.

Woodenhead can disturb – Gert writhes in mangroves and wears strange underwear; the Princess is kidnapped by Gustav the Strongman – but also uplift. 'Lucky Star' and 'Hospice for Destitute Lovers' are tender off-key elegies and as a love story the film is full of la douleur exquise.

Although one critic asked if *Woodenhead* had been filmed on the moon, the sensuous landscape is Northland. A digital camera was used – no funder in their right mind would have given money for a shoot-on-negative – but the film is no worse for it. The gorgeous black and white cinematography finds unexpected textures.

Habicht has said that being able to mix photography, humour, soft pornography, music, storytelling and experimentation drew him to film-making. Add folktale, dance, vandalism and donkey and you have *Woodenhead*.

Woodenhead
2003 / Feature / 90 mins

DIRECTOR / PRODUCER / SCREENPLAY / **Florian Habicht**
PRODUCTION COMPANY / **Pictures For Anna**

The World's Fastest Indian

THIS BIOPIC OF INVERCARGILL'S BURT MUNRO, the back-shed genius who adapted a 1920s Indian Scout motorcycle to try and break the world speed record, is as uncomplicated and straightforward as Munro's machine. There are no fireworks, nor do there need to be, although a sequence on Oreti Beach when Burt's motorcycle finally fires and hares past leather-clad bikies is as exhilarating for the viewer as it must have been for the rider.

Roger Donaldson had wanted to make this film since 1971 when he worked on *Offerings To The God Of Speed*, a documentary about Munro. Waylaid in Hollywood directing films such as *Cocktail* and *Dante's Peak*, he took two decades to return to New Zealand and fulfill the dream. His lengthy obsession has parallels with Munro's single-minded pursuit of the world record on Utah's Bonneville Salt Flats.

Arriving in Los Angeles en route to Utah, Munro is the archetypal innocent in the big city who overcomes hurdles by being charming and non-judgemental. A transsexual helps him with customs difficulties. A widow on a farm helps him with his car (and a little more). And at Bonneville everybody helps him.

There is not much character development – Munro simply goes from laconic, genial outsider to successful laconic, genial outsider.

The World's Fastest Indian
2005 / Feature / 126 mins

DIRECTOR / SCREENPLAY / **Roger Donaldson**
PRODUCERS / **Gary Hannam, Roger Donaldson**
PRODUCTION COMPANY / **WFI Productions**

Nor is there a lot of conflict, apart from his neighbours in Invercargill despairing at his revving engines, feral yard, and fixation with urinating on a lemon tree. But there is captivating narrative drive. Both plot and engine casings hot up when Munro gets to Speed Week at Bonneville. The outcome may be inevitable, but Munro's attempts to break the record on his antique two-wheeler and his inevitable failures to stay vertical are marvellously filmed and riveting.

The film has excellent cameos from Annie Whittle and Diane Ladd as two of Burt's lovers, and the mayor of Invercargill, Tim Shadbolt, as, well, the mayor of Invercargill. Anthony Hopkins (*Silence Of The Lambs, Shadowlands*), gives one of the most understated performances of his career as Munro, complete with southern burr, and Munro's family was moved to tears when they visited the set.

But this is no overwrought hagiography. When one of Munro's speed contemporaries, American John Rice, was asked whether the man was as nice as he is portrayed in the movie, he replied, 'No, he was even nicer.'

The films in this book span more than a century – the earliest, *The Departure Of The Second Contingent For The Boer War*, a precious remnant of just 45 seconds, was made in 1900. You won't find this – and many other films featured in this book – at your local video store. Don't despair, however: there are many ways you can view them.

- **New Zealand Film Archive.** Details over page.
- **Online**. Some films – particularly shorts – can be viewed via the internet. Try **New Zealand Onscreen** (www.nzonscreen.org.nz) and the **New Zealand Film Archive** (www.filmarchive.org.nz). The **New Zealand Film Commission** has its own **You Tube** site for short films (www.youtube.com/nzfilmshorts), and others may be available on You Tube via a general search.
- **Aro Street Video Shop** (www.arovideo.co.nz; 97 Aro Street, Wellington, tel/fax +64 (4) 801-7101.) Based in Wellington, this store holds the biggest collection of New Zealand films for both rental (including mail-order rental) and purchase. Films can be searched in the online catalogue.
- **Your local video store**. Some video stores do hold copies of New Zealand films, particularly recent or enduringly popular titles.
- **iTunes**. In the future, some films may be available for purchase on iTunes. One, *Tama Tu*, is already on iTunes US.
- **Public libraries.** It is also worth trying your public library; some libraries hold New Zealand films on video or DVD format. Many have online catalogues.

The New Zealand Film Archive
Nga Kaitiaki O Nga Taonga Whitiahua

Most of the films in this book can be viewed at Film Archive libraries in Auckland and Wellington. Check the website www.filmarchive.org.nz for the online catalogue, as well as news and special events.

Wellington Media Library,
New Zealand Film Archive
Cnr Ghuznee & Taranaki Streets
Te Aro
Wellington 6011
Tel (04) 384-7647
Open: Mon–Fri, 12pm–5pm

Auckland Office,
New Zealand Film Archive
Level 1, 300 Karangahape Road
Newton, Auckland 1010
Tel (09) 379-0688
Open: Mon–Fri 11am–5pm,
Sat 11am–4pm

At the time of this book's publication, some films from the Archive's collections could be viewed at the following galleries, museums and libraries. Please check with the organisation concerned for up-to-date information.

Whangarei District Library, tel (09) 430-4206,
www.whangarei-libraries.com
Hamilton City Library, tel (07) 838-6826,
www.hamiltonlibraries.co.nz
Govett-Brewster Art Gallery, New Plymouth, tel (06) 759-6060,
www.govettbrewster.com
Te Wananga-o-Raukawa, Otaki, tel (06) 364-9011, www.twor.ac.nz
Te Puna Toi (in the Arts Centre), Christchurch, tel (03) 365-3159,
www.tafs.canterbury.ac.nz/tepunatoi
Dunedin Public Art Gallery, tel (03) 477-4000,
http://dunedin.art.museum
Otago Settlers Museum, tel (03) 477-5052,
www.otago.settlers.museum

Acknowledgements

Writing a book, like making a film, is a collaborative effort. The following people and places have contributed substantially to what you hold in your hands: Helga Arlington, Wanganui District Library, Andrew Fieldsend, Peter Tait, Videon, Andrew Armitage at Aro St. Video Shop, New Zealand Film Archive, especially Mark Williams, Mark Sweeney, Amelia Harris, Siobhan Garrett, Kathy Dudding and David Coventry, Jane O'Loughlin, Andrew McDouall, Environment Centre, Jack Riddet Tripe, Rachael King, Mark Raffety, Shirley and Gerald McDouall, Shaun Pulman, Steve at Civic Video Mt Eden, Juliette Veber, Bill Toepfer, Duncan Petrie, Fiona Carroll, George Rose, Richard Adams, Gina Dellabarca, Hugh MacDonald, Bob Stenhouse, Michael Heath, Heather Randerson, John McRae, Peter Burger, Campbell Walker, Dan Slevin, Miles Buckingham, Vapi Kupenga, Jeff Simmonds, Ross T. Smith, Nick Bollinger, Amanda Carter, Martin Rumsby, Rosemary Riddell, Alister Barry, Grant Ogilvie, Russell Campbell, Kate Lange, Don and Elizabeth McRae, and Alex Galvin.

For images I thank Kiri Griffin at the Film Archive, Jasmin McSweeney and Lucy Cleary at the New Zealand Film Commission, John Bell, Tyler Cann, Marc Chesterman, Jan Chapman Films, James Cunningham, Phil Dadson, John Davies, Rachel Davies, Rhys Duncan, Sharon Duncan, Uili Fectau at Archives New Zealand, Catherine Fitzgerald, Victoria Ginn, Annie Goldson, David Hughes, Owen Hughes, Sam Kelly, Ruth Kaupua, Grant Lahood, Merata Mita, Anthony Phelps, Leanne Pooley, Gaylene Preston, Paddy Reilly, David Robertson, South Pacific Pictures, Paul Swadel, John Toon, Michelle Turner, Television New Zealand, Vincent Ward, Taika Waititi, Evan Webb, Peter Wells, and Sebastian Meek at WingNut Films.

Thanks to my wife Elinor, who has borne this project heavily and almost always patiently. And incredible gratitude to Mary Varnham and Sarah Bennett of Awa Press.

Illustrations

All photo IDs from left to right unless otherwise stated.

An Angel At My Table p. 5: Kerry Fox, Stills Collection, New Zealand Film Archive Nga Kaitiaki O Nga Taonga Whitiatua; p. 6: Kerry Fox, courtesy New Zealand Film Commission Te Tumu Whakaata Taonga **Angel Mine** p. 8: courtesy New Zealand Film Commission **Avondale Dogs** p. 10: Melinni Blake, courtesy New Zealand Film Commission **Baby Farmer** p. 12: Kylie O'Callaghan and Phil Vaughan, courtesy Sam Kelly **Bad Blood** p. 14: Jack Thompson and Carol Burns; p. 15: Bruce Allpress (left), and Ian Watkin (right), Renown Productions Ltd **Beautiful** pp. 16 & 17: Jason Hoyte and Tim Gordon, courtesy New Zealand Film Commission **Beyond Reasonable Doubt** p. 18: Diana Rowan, John Hargreaves and David Hemmings, courtesy Endeavour Productions Limited, Stills Collection, New Zealand Film Archive **Blue Willow** p. 21: courtesy New Zealand Film Commission **Braindead** p. 23: Tina Regtien and Jed Brophy, WingNut Films Productions Limited **Broken Barrier** p. 25: Kay Ngarimu and Terence Bayler, Stills Collection, New Zealand Film Archive **Came A Hot Friday** p. 27: Billy T. James; p. 28: Phillip Gordon, Stills Collection, New Zealand Film Archive **The Coaster** p. 30: National Film Unit Collection, Archives New Zealand **A Colour Box** p. 32: Len Lye, still from A Colour Box, 1935 (3 min, 35mm, Gasparcolour, sound), courtesy Len Lye Foundation, The British Post Office, Govett-Brewster Art Gallery and the New Zealand Film Archive **Crush** p. 35: Marcia Gay Harden, courtesy New Zealand Film Commission **A Death In The Family** p. 37: Simon Prast, Ray Edkins and Vivienne Laube, courtesy Peter Wells, photograph Bede Stevens **The Departure Of The Second Contingent For The Boer War** p. 39: Stills Collection, New Zealand Film Archive **Derek** p. 41: Ian Mune **Desperate Rem-**

edies p. 43: Cliff Curtis, Kevin Smith, Jennifer Ward-Lealand and Lisa Chappell, Stills Collection, New Zealand Film Archive **Drum/Sing** p. 45: (top) Wayne Laird, (bottom) Phil Dadson; p. 46: courtesy Phil Dadson, photographs Wally Floyd **The End Of The Golden Weather** p. 48: Poster Collection, New Zealand Film Archive **The Feathers Of Peace** p. 50: Rei Samuels, Stills Collection, New Zealand Film Archive **Flying Fox In A Freedom Tree** p. 53: Richard von Sturmer and Faifua Amiga, courtesy New Zealand Film Commission **Footage** p. 5: courtesy Owen Hughes, photographs Anne Shelton **Forgotten Silver** p. 57 scene from *Salome*; p. 58: Colin McKenzie [sic], Stills Collection, New Zealand Film Archive **Fracture** p. 60: Jared Turner and Kate Elliot, courtesy New Zealand Film Commission **Free Radicals** p. 62: Len Lye, still from Free Radicals, 1958 (4 min, 16mm, black & white, sound), image copyright Len Lye Foundation, courtesy Govett-Brewster Art Gallery and New Zealand Film Archive **The Frog, The Dog And The Devil** p. 64: TVNZ Television Archive **A Game With No Rules** p. 65: Jennifer Ward-Lealand; p. 66: Marton Csokas and Danielle Cormack, courtesy New Zealand Film Commission **Gone Up North For A While** p. 68: Paul Holmes and Denise Maunder, National Film Unit Collection, Archives New Zealand **Goodbye Pork Pie** p. 70: (top) Kelly Johnson and Tony Barry, Stills Collection, New Zealand Film Archive ; p. 71: courtesy New Zealand Film Commission **Haunting Douglas** p. 73: Douglas Wright and Lisa Denson, courtesy Leanne Pooley, photograph Peter Molloy **Heavenly Creatures** p. 75: Kate Winslet and Melanie Lynskey, Pierre Vinet/Courtesy of Miramax Film Corp. **I Want To Be Joan** p. 78: courtesy Stephanie Beth **Illustrious Energy** p. 80: Shaun Bao, Stills Collection, New Zealand Film Archive **In My Father's Den** p. 81 and p.82: Matthew Macfadyen and Emily Barclay, courtesy New Zealand Film Commission **In Spring One Plants Alone** p. 84: Puhi, courtesy New Zealand Film Commission **Infection** pp. 86 &

87: Supercollider Ltd **Jack Be Nimble** p. 89: Alexis Arquette and Sarah Smuts-Kennedy, courtesy New Zealand Film Commission **Kaikohe Demolition** pp. 91 & 92: photographs Frank Habicht **King-pin** p. 94: Poster Collection, New Zealand Film Archive; p. 95: Nicholas Rogers (right), Stills Collection, New Zealand Film Archive; **Kitchen Sink** p. 97: Theresa Healey and Peter Tait, courtesy New Zealand Film Commission **The Little Things** p. 99: Norissa Taia, courtesy New Zealand Film Commission **The Lord Of The Rings** p. 101: Miranda Otto, New Line Productions, Inc. The Saul Zaentz Company d/b/a Tolkien Enterprises under licence to New Line Productions, Inc. All Rights Reserved **The Lounge Bar** p. 104: (top) Don McGlashan, (bottom) Lucy Sheehan and Harry Sinclair, Stills Collection, New Zealand Film Archive **Lovelock** p. 106: Crispin Balfour and Andrew Couling, courtesy David Robertson, photograph Kerry Brown **Magik And Rose** p. 108: Nicola Murphy and Alison Bruce, Stills Collection, New Zealand Film Archive **The Maori Merchant of Venice** p. 110: Ngarimu Daniels and Te Rangihau Gilbert, p. 111: Te Rangihau Gilbert and Sonny Kirikiri, He Taonga Films **Meet The Feebles** pp. 112 & 113: WingNut Films Productions Limited **Memory And Desire** p. 115: Yuri Kinugawa and Eugene Nomura, courtesy New Zealand Film Commission **Middle Age Spread** p. 117: Grant Tilly, courtesy Endeavour Productions Ltd, Stills Collection, New Zealand Film Archive **Mr Wrong** p. 119: Heather Bolton; p. 120: David Letch, courtesy Gaylene Preston, photographs David Hamilton **The Navigator: A Medieval Odyssey** p. 122: Bruce Lyons, p. 123: Hamish McFarlane, courtesy New Zealand Film Commission **The Newest City On The Globe** p. 125: Marise Creagh, Leon Narbey and Rick Allender, courtesy Peter Wells, photograph Chris Matthews **Ngati** p. 127: (top) Ross Girven and Wi Kuki Kaa, (bottom) Judy McIntosh and Connie Pewhairangi, Stills Collection, New Zealand Film Archive; p. 128: courtesy New Zealand Film Commission **Once**

Were Warriors p. 130: (clockwise from top left) Rena Owen, Cliff Curtis, Temuera Morrison and Mamaengaroa Kerr-Bell, Communicado Features **Out Of The Blue** p. 133: Matt Sunderland, courtesy New Zealand Film Commission **Patu!** pp. 134 & 135: Anthony Phelps **The Piano** p. 139: Holly Hunter and Anna Paquin, Jan Chapman Films/TF1 International **Punitive Damage** p. 141: Kamal Bamadhaj and friends, photograph Alison Murray; p. 142 (top) photograph Steven Cox, (bottom) Ruth Todd, photograph Ann Shelton **The Quiet Earth** p. 144: Bruno Lawrence, Stills Collection, New Zealand Film Archive; p. 145: courtesy New Zealand Film Commission **Rain** p. 147: (top) Sarah Pierse, (bottom) Aaron Murphy; p. 148: Alicia Fulford-Wierzbicki and Sarah Pierse, courtesy Rose Road **Rain Of The Children** p. 149: Miriama Rangi; p. 150: courtesy New Zealand Film Commission **The Road Back** p. 153: Ana Jankovits and John Watson, courtesy New Zealand Film Commission **Ruby And Rata** p. 155: Lee Mete-Kingi and Yvonne Lawley, courtesy Gaylene Preston, photograph Geoff Short **Runaway** p. 157: Colin Broadley and Deidre McCarron, Stills Collection, New Zealand Film Archive **The Sadness Of The Post-Intellectual Art Critic** p. 159: George Rose, courtesy George Rose **The Scarecrow** p. 161: Jonathan Smith and Daniel McLaren; p. 162: (left) John Carradine, (right) Tracey Mann, Stills Collection, New Zealand Film Archive **Second-Hand Wedding** p. 163: Geraldine Brophy and Tina Regtien; p. 164: Ryan O'Kane and Holly Shanahan, photographs Paddy Reilly, www.paddyreilly.com **The Singing Trophy** pp. 166 & 167: Peter Tait, courtesy Keir and Cox Productions **Sione's Wedding** p. 169: Iaheto Ah Hi, Oscar Kightley, Shimpal Lelisi and Robbie Magasiva, South Pacific Pictures, photograph Kirsty Griffin **Skin Deep** p. 171: Deryn Cooper, Stills Collection, New Zealand Film Archive **Sleeping Dogs** p. 173: Sam Neill; p. 175: Stills Collection, New Zealand Film Archive **A Small Life** p. 176: Mahinarangi Tocker, courtesy Michael Heath, photograph Bhim Singh Chouhan **Smash Palace** p. 179: Greer Robson and Bruno Lawrence; p. 180: Stills Collection, New Zealand Film Archive **Snakeskin** p. 182: Melanie Lynskey; p. 183: Dean O'Gorman, Boyd Kestner and Melanie Lynskey, courtesy New Zealand Film Commission **Someone Else's Country** p. 185: Roger Douglas and David Lange, Alexander Turnbull Library (EP/1987/4138/26), Wellington, photograph Ross Giblin **Stickmen** p. 187: Robbie Magasiva; p. 188: Anne Nordhaus and Simone Kessell; p. 189: Scott Wills, Robbie Magasiva and Paolo Rotondo, courtesy Michelle Turner, photographs Guy Robinson **Still Life** p. 191: June Bishop and Joseph Hancox, courtesy New Zealand Film Commission **Strike Zone** p. 193: Cameron Duncan, *New Zealand Herald*, photograph Glenn Jeffrey **Sweetness** p. 194: Rachel Davies, courtesy Tim Rose/Rachel Davies **Take 3** p. 196: Li-Ming Hu, Michelle Ang and Katlyn Wong, photograph Briar March, courtesy New Zealand Film Commission **Talkback** p. 199: Lucy Sheehan, courtesy New Zealand Film Commission **Tama Tu** p. 201: (bottom) Tammy Davis, courtesy Aio Films/Defender Films Ltd **The Te Kooti Trail** p. 203: Patiti Warbrick and Tina Hunt; p. 204: Hayward Collection, New Zealand Film Archive **This Is New Zealand** p. 206: National Film Unit Collection, Archives New Zealand **Tongan Ninja** p. 209: Linda Tseng and Sione Finau, courtesy New Zealand Film Commission **Topless Women Talk About Their Lives** p. 211: Shimpal Lelisi, Ian Hughes, Willa O'Neill, Joel Toebeck, Danielle Cormack, courtesy New Zealand Film Commission **The Topp Twins: Untouchable Girls** p. 213: Lynda Topp and Jools Topp, photograph Sally Tagg **Turangawaewae/A Place To Stand** p. 215: Nancy Brunning and Wi Kuki Kaa, courtesy Blueskin Films, photograph Rewa Harre **Two Cars, One Night** p. 217: Rangi Ngamoki and Te Ahiwaru Ngamoki-Richards, courtesy New Zealand Film Commission **Utu** p. 219: Anzac Wallace, courtesy Victoria Ginn, Stills Collection, New Zealand Film Archive **A Very Nice Honeymoon** pp.

221 & 222: courtesy New Zealand Film Commission **Vigil** p. 224: Frank Whitten and Fiona Kay, Stills Collection, New Zealand Film Archive **The Waimate Conspiracy** p. 227: Jim Moriarty, photograph Bruce Hutton **Walkshort** p. 229: Don McGlashan and Harry Sinclair, courtesy New Zealand Film Commission **War Stories Our Mothers Never Told Us** p. 231: (clockwise from top left) Tui Preston, Pamela Quill, Jean Andrews, Neva Clarke McKenna, Judith Fyfe, Flo Small, Rita Graham, Mabel Waititi and Gaylene Preston, courtesy Gaylene Preston, photograph Jane Ussher **Whale Rider** p. 233: Keisha Castle-Hughes and Rawiri Paratene; p. 234: Keisha Castle-Hughes, South Pacific Pictures Limited/ApolloMedia GmbH & Co 5 Filmproduktion KG 2002, photographer Kirsty Griffin **Why Can't I Stop This Uncontrollable Dancing?** p. 236: Nia Robyn, courtesy Campbell Walker **Woodenhead** p. 237: Georgie Hill; p: 238: Teresa Peters and Matthew Sunderland; p. 239: Nicholas Butler, photographs Chris Pryor **The World's Fastest Indian** pp. 240 and 241: Anthony Hopkins; p. 243, courtesy New Zealand Film Commission.

The author and publisher have endeavoured to acknowledge correctly all illustrations. Any errors or omissions brought to our attention will be rectified in subsequent printings.

Index

Page references in italics refer to illustrations.

T